AF541744

ESSAYS ON TEACHING MATHEMATICS

Books by **Marlow Ediger** *and*
Digumarti Bhaskara Rao

Administration of Schools
Community Colleges
Curriculum Organisation
Curriculum of School Subjects
Effective Schooling
Effective School Curriculum
Elementary Curriculum
Elementary Curriculum Improvement
Essays on Teaching Mathematics
Essays on Teaching Science
Essays on Teaching Social Studies
Essays on Teaching Reading
Essays on Teaching and Learning
Improving School Administration
Issues in School Curriculum
Language Arts Curriculum
Philosophy and Curriculum
Psychology and Curriculum
Quality School Education
Reading Curriculum and Instruction
Relevancy in Elementary Curriculum
School Organisation
School Curriculum and Administration
Science Curriculum
Teaching English Successfully
Teaching Language Arts Successfully
Teaching Mathematics Successfully
Teaching Science Successfully
Teaching Social Studies Successfully
Teaching Mathematics in Elementary Schools
Teaching Science in Elementary Schools
Successful School Administration
Successful School Education

published by
Discovery Publishing House

ESSAYS ON TEACHING MATHEMATICS

by

Dr. Marlow Ediger
Emeritus Professor of Education
Truman State University
P.O. Box 417, 201 W 22nd St
North Newton KS 67117
United States of America

and

Dr. Digumarti Bhaskara Rao
Reader and Research Director
R.V.R. College of Education
D-43 (277) S.V.N. Colony
Guntur-522006, India

DISCOVERY PUBLISHING HOUSE PVT. LTD.
NEW DELHI-110 002

Published by:
Tilak Wasan
DISCOVERY PUBLISHING HOUSE PVT. LTD.
4383/4B, Ansari Road, Darya Ganj
New Delhi-110 002 (India)
Phone : +91-11-23279245, 43596064-65
Fax : +91-11-23253475
E-mail : discoverypublishinghouse@gmail.com
sales@discoverypublishinggroup.com
web : www.discoverypublishinggroup.com

First Edition: **2011**

Reprinted: **2017**

ISBN: 978-81-8356-880-7

Essays on Teaching Mathematics

Printed at:
Infinity Imaging Systems
Delhi

dedicated
to

Harshitha and Sarat Chandra
7607 Huckleberry Way SE, Snoqualmie, WA98065, USA

Preface

Mathematics is the study of quantity, structure, space, and change. Mathematics seeks out patterns, formulates new conjectures, and establishes truth by rigorous deduction from appropriately chosen axioms and definitions. Mathematics is used throughout the world as an essential tool in many fields, including natural science, engineering, medicine, and the social sciences. Applied mathematics, the branch of mathematics concerned with application of mathematical knowledge to other fields, inspires and makes use of new mathematical discoveries and sometimes leads to the development of entirely new mathematical disciplines, such as statistics and game theory. Mathematicians also engage in pure mathematics, or mathematics for its own sake, without having any application in mind, although practical applications for what began as pure mathematics are often discovered. Now the teaching of Mathematics is made a school subject across the world and such subject needs successful teaching.

In the successful teaching of mathematics, the teaching learning equipment the administrator, the teacher, the curriculum, the library, the mathemetics laboratories, the academic atmosphere, the teaching-learning programmes, etc., play their legitimate role.

This book will be of great use to curriculum designers and teachers and administrators.

Digumarti Bhaskara Rao
digumartibhaskararao@redeiffmail.com

Sri Sai Soudha
D-43 S.V.N. Colony
Guntur 522006
India

Contents

Preface

1. Mathematics : Content and Pedagogy 1
2. Psychological Foundations in Teaching Mathematics 7
3. Trends in Teaching Mathematics 14
4. Problems in Teaching Mathematics 20
5. Quality Teaching in Mathematics 27
6. Direct Teaching vs Constructivism in Mathematics 33
7. Substitute Teacher and Mathematics Curriculum 39
8. Mathematics Curriculum and Psychology of Learning 45
9. Quality in Mathematics Curriculum 53
10. Data Driven Decision-making in Mathematics 59
11. Collaboration in Improving Mathematics Curriculum 65
12. Factors that Assist Mathematics Achievement 71
13. Portfolios in Mathematics Curriculum 78
14. Enjoyment in Mathematics Curriculum 85
15. Computer-aided Instruction in Mathematics Curriculum 92
16. Reading in Mathematics Curriculum 99

Additional Reading 105

Index 129

1

CHAPTER

Mathematics : Content and Pedagogy

The debate has gone on for some time in terms of which is more salient for the teacher to be well versed in mathematical content versus methods and approaches in teaching. Both are salient. They cannot be separated from each other. The mathematics teacher must indeed have broad, indepth knowledge of subject matter as well as in teaching and learning. Mathematical content and pedagogy then need to be integrated. The goal of mathematics teachers is to assist pupils to achieve, grow, and develop in attaining vital facts, concepts, and generalizations. This takes teacher knowledge of content as well as of pedagogy.

Teaching of Mathematics

There are several needs of individuals in becoming proficient in mathematics. Thus, each person needs to be able to use mathematics in everyday transactions such as buying necessary goods and services. To buy groceries, pay utility bills and rent, and pay for needed services such as repairs and maintenance work. Functioning well, numerically, in society is a need for all citizens. Then too, a mathematics curriculum must provide for those going into higher education and will major in and teach mathematics. Also, there will be future engineers and other professionals who need to experience a high quality school curriculum. Individual differences then must be provided for in the elementary and secondary school years. Sequentially, pupils need to experience teachers who possess ample knowledge of subject-matter as well as of methods of teaching mathematics (Ediger and Rao, 2000).

Quality teachers are needed, as a key ingredient, in assisting optimal pupil learning. They must experience the latest, relevant trends in teaching mathematics, be it in workshops, other inservice education programmes, or through personal research projects. Cooperation among teachers to conduct grade level meetings as well as school wide, and system wide endeavors at curriculum improvement should provide for provisions made for optimal achievement in mathematics of each learner. Here, content and pedagogy need integration in helping pupils achieve well. The two should not be separated from each other, nor should value judgments be made as to which is more important (Ediger, 2005).

Mathematics as a language needs to be used to communicate ideas. Communication must occur in school and in society between and among individuals pertaining to quantitative topics. Precision is involved. Mathematics is perhaps the most objective of all academic disciplines whereby individuals agree, as a whole, with the quantity being discussed. It attempts to be precise with the quantity being considered. Among others, mathematical ideas may be expressed orally and in diagrams, charts, tables, formulas, library books, graphs, and written work (See Betne and Castonguay, 2008).

Pupils need to make connections in terms of use of mathematical subject matter. They need to perceive how mathematics relates to the self, as well as others. Problem solving is a vital skill for all to develop. Developmentally and at increasing levels of difficulty, pupils must be able to solve personal mathematics problems. Logical thinking is necessary here as well as dealing factually with quantitative information. Critical thinking is inherent when separating facts from opinions, the relevant from the non-relevant, as well as fantasy from reality in problem solving experiences. Creative thinking, too, is necessary in determining new methods of solving a problem. Novel, unique ways of viewing and attempting solutions at problem solving are to be encouraged (Stein, 2007).

Contextual situations are needed in fostering the utilization of mathematics. Standardized tests stress the application of mathematics outside the framework of a particular context. Pupils then respond to test items which do not pinpoint a functional use. Then too, pupils are drilled much to do well on a standardized test. Generally, drill assists pupils in turning off in studying mathematics. Mathematics can be made into a fascinating academic discipline with the solving of life like problems whereby pupils may see its use in society. Challenging and interesting methods may be used to stimulate pupil interest in learning mathematics. Mathematics certainly need not be dull and uninteresting. Actually, it should be enjoyable and fascinating. New objectives need to be built upon what pupils have learned previously (National Council Teachers of Mathematics, 2000).

There are diverse kinds of knowledge that teachers need to teach mathematics to pupils and include knowledge of :

- subject-matter including important principles and meanings, formulas, facts, processes and procedures, rules, definitions, as well as structural ideas.
- pedagogy such as lesson and unit planning and implementation, questions to ask and problems to solve, explanations to use, examples to provide as in diagrams and formulas, and demonstrations to make situations meaningful and concrete.

- pedagogical subject-matter including determining prerequisites pupils possess prior to instruction, sequence used to develop vital mathematical understandings among learners, diagnosis of pupil difficulties in learning, as well as strategies to use with quality materials of instruction (Jeyanthi, 2008).
- information about pupils in the classroom. Here, the teacher needs to understand the developmental level of each pupil and where he/she is achieving presently. The teacher should not impart content too difficult, nor to easy for learner attainment. Thus, the subject matter to be imparted needs to be challenging, yet achievable. The learning styles of pupils need to be considered in teaching and learning situations. Thus, a pupil may prefer direct teaching of content as compared to learning by discovery. He/she may prefer to work by the self instead of in collaborative situations. Then too, pupils may prefer a textbook approach as compared to more open ended procedures in using a variety of activities and experiences.
- curriculum development, curriculum practices and procedures. Mathematics teachers need to develop proficiency in writing cognitive, psychomotor, and affective objectives for pupil attainment. These must be written in measurable terms to ascertain if they have/ have not been achieved by learners. Diagnosis is then possible to determine which learning activities are necessary for pupils to remedy deficits. A variety of valid, reliable measurement procedures need to be used to determine pupil progress. Multiple choice and essay test items, among others may then be emphasized (National Council Teachers of Mathematics, 1989).

The mathematics teacher then must appraise the self to notice if there are personal strengths in mathematics to effectively emphasize the scope and sequence of needed math in the curriculum to teach effectively. Inservice education may take care of deficiencies since what is not known may not be taught or be taught well for pupil understanding and meaning. The goal of teachers here should be to obtain a master's degree in mathematics as a minimum. Online education is also possible to work at home, at one's own convenience, in taking additional course work in mathematics knowledge and pedagogy. School sponsored workshops, and attending professional meetings, are further avenues of inservice education. The principles of educational psychology must be stressed adequately in course work dealing with imparting mathematical knowledge to pupils (Hyde, 2006).

The Attitudinal Dimension in Teaching Mathematics

The self-concept of the teacher is of utmost importance. He/she must believe in the worth of the individual. This is true in believing in one self as well as in others. The following traits of teachers are salient when thinking of teaching mathematics :

- possessing a good attitude toward mathematics as an academic discipline.
- having positive attitudes toward teaching in general and teaching mathematics, in particular.
- inculcating a philosophy of teaching which accepts research results as a guide to teaching.
- enjoying mathematics as an area of study as well as in imparting knowledge, skills, and attitudes toward pupils.
- wanting to become increasingly proficient in teaching mathematics.
- desiring to attend workshop sessions, to take courses in mathematics/pedagogy, as well as in the psychology of teaching and learning.
- emphasizing a positive relationship with parents in assisting their offspring to do well in mathematics, as well as in school in general.

The attitudinal dimension is further emphasized in classroom management procedures. The mathematics teacher must have a quality classroom environment for teaching and learning. Pupils are respected and yet learners are mannerly when relating to others. The teacher has reasonable expectations from pupils in goal attainment. Successful achievement is salient for each pupil. Teachers are able to work well with pupils in large group, cooperative endeavors, and in individualized instruction. Emotional achievement is important for every one in the classroom, in school, and in society (Glatthorn and Fox, 1996).

References

Betne, Praha, and Remi Castonguay (2008), "On the Role of Mathematics Educators and Librarians in Constructive Pedagogy," *Education,* 129 (1), 56-79.

Ediger, Marlow (2005), "Teaching Mathematics in the High School Setting," *College Student Journal*, 39 (4), 711-715.

Ediger, Marlow, and D. Bhaskara Rao (2000), *Teaching Mathematics Successfully*. New Delhi, India: Discovery Publishing House.

Glatthorn, A. A., and L. E. Fox, (1996), *Quality Teaching Through Professional Development*. Thousand Oaks, CA: Corwin Press.

Hyde, A. A. (2006), Comprehending Math: Adapting Strategies to Teach Mathematics K-6. Portsmouth, NH: Heinemann.

Jeyanthi, S. (2008), Cognitive and Attitudinal Correlates of Teaching Performance of B. Ed. Mathematics Teachers. Kodaikanal, India: Mother Teresa Women's University, 41-48. Ph D thesis appraised by the writer in serving as an External Examiner for Mother Teresa University.

National Council Teachers of Mathematics (2000), *Principles and Standards for School Mathematics*. Reston, Va.: NCTM.

National Council Teachers of Mathematics (1989), Curriculum and Evaluation Standards for School Mathematics. Reston, Va.: NCTM.

Stein, Lynn Arthur 2007), "How Mathematics Counts," *Educational Leadership*, 65 (3), 9-14.

2

CHAPTER

Psychological Foundations in Teaching Mathematics

There are selected foundational ideas in teaching which all mathematics teachers need to endorse. When following these ideas, teachers should be able to assist in greater learner achievement. There are problems faced by teachers in securing student engagement in ongoing lessons in mathematics. Motivation is then lacking to make progress in the mathematics curriculum. Student optimal achievement is necessary from each day's lesson; otherwise a student lacks sequential learnings which provide readiness for ensuing lessons in mathematics (Ediger, 2005).

Reasons for Lack of Student Achievement

There are salient reasons for students lacking achievement in ongoing lessons and units of study. Each mathematics teacher must diagnose and ascertain reasons why a student is not making adequate progress (Ediger and Rao, 2001). Selected reasons may well come under the following categories:

- **entry behaviours for achieving a new objective.** A student then is not ready to benefit from the new learning activities. The ensuing subject matter then does not relate to previous content acquired. The perception of the student fails to perceive the connections. The lack of perceived relationships prevents understanding of the new content being presented. The mathematics teacher needs to be certain that students possess the prerequisites to benefit from the ensuing lesson/unit of study. It may be necessary to teach ordered activities to take care of the deficiency. Through teacher observation, the mathematics teacher may notice learner deficiencies and remedy these in order that learners possess the needed entry behaviors (Ediger, 2007).

- **conceptual errors necessary to achieve and make progress.** Which concepts do students fail to understand? Through discussions, the student might well reveal what is vague and hazy. Here, the teacher must take notice of these relevant concepts for remedial as well as for ensuing lessons and units of study. Lack of conceptual understanding of the commutative, associative, and distributive properties, for example, might well cause learner difficulties when solving word problems. Concepts need to be understand contextually within a variety of rich learning experiences. Students must use these concepts meaningfully in the mathematics curriculum in order to retain their meanings and to enhance learning. Mathematics concepts need to be presented in practical situations. Mathematics is utilitarian in that uses can be made of it in school and in society (Ediger, 2002).
- **computational errors which provide a basis for sequential learnings.** Computational errors accrue due to carelessness, haste in completing an assignment, incorrect understandings, and a lack of meaningful learning experiences. Proofing one's work cuts down on computational errors. Errors still are possible due to a lack of not having mastered skills in basic

operations on number. Whatever the cause of computational errors, these need diagnosis and remediation. With the use of developmental^ appropriate manipulative materials, audio visual aids, computerized programs, duplicated materials, and abstract learnings from textbooks and workbooks, students with teacher assistance may progress sequentially. Interest factors for learning are salient when choosing materials of instruction. Establishing purpose for learning in computation endeavors also assists in guiding optimal student achievement. Students then accept reasons for ongoing lessons. Students need to understand the "why" and the "how" of computing (Savithiri, 2006).

Attitudes and Student Mathematics Achievement

With good attitudes, student achievement in mathematics may well be enhanced. Mathematics teachers and students then need to develop concepts pertaining to self efficacy (Bandura, 1977). Efficacious teachers tend to be more open to new, quality ideas in teaching, including the use of inquiry methods, as well as taking risks in trying out new ideas in the instructional arena. Self-efficacy emphasizes judgments made by the individual pertaining to his/her abilities to accomplish certain levels of performance. Self-efficacy beliefs govern much of human functioning and mediate how individuals think, feel, motivate themselves. Thus, a teacher assists students to achieve well regardless of of external factors such the home/family situation or the school and class environments (Swars, 2005).

The self-concept then becomes highly significant in teaching and learning situations. The teacher who has confidence in his/her abilities to assist learners to do well in mathematics regardless of the latters personal traits, abilities, and charac-teristics is a much wanted professional. There are a plethora of data on a student's profile which assist in determining achievement and progress. These include the following :

- possessing mathematical intelligence, (Gardner, 1993).
- personal styles of learning (Searson and Dunn, 2001).
- maturational level of the student (Piaget, 1950).
- interests possessed.
- purposes for and in learning as to what is deemed to be salient.
- cultural factors in what is perceived to be important (Author's Footnote).
- readiness for learning in mathematics, including background experiences.
- socio-economic factors.

Self-efficacy theorists believe that mathematics teachers might well rise above each of the above items to assist students to achieve optimally. The last item with an asterisk has been researched numerous times. Students from middle class neighborhoods achieve considerably higher than those from low income homes. Poverty seemingly hinders students from doing well academically. More privileged homes provide many opportunities for promoting learner progresses as compared to poverty situations. Thus, more comfortable homes, non-formal educational opportunities, travel, safe and clean neighborhoods, quality transportation, adequate nutritious foods, good clothing, and adequate medical/dental care are much more available to middle class homes as compared to low income areas.

Cooperative Learning in Mathematics

Managing a classroom of learners is indeed challenging to the teacher. Students may work individually, such as an assignment from a basal mathematics textbook. Good teaching may accrue here when student interest and meaning is attached to the lesson. Readiness, too, must be added to the assignment having merit.

Small group work may also be stressed in classroom management as in cooperative learning. Here, students may work together in pooling ideas for problem solving. Each shared idea is evaluated and assessed. By working together harmoniously, students might well accomplish the goal of solving a mathematical problem, in which critical and creative thinking were emphasized. The small group needs to work together and not in competition with each other. Group efforts, here, involve pooling of ideas to arrive at a solution.

Vygotsky (1934, 1986) stressed a social theory of learning whereby students learned from each other in committee settings. As students in the small group setting discuss the solving of a mathematical problem, each contributes in possibilities. Students then learn from each other in a social setting. Vygotsky, too, emphasized the zone of proximal development. The zone represents a gap between where the student is presently in achievement and a higher ideal or objective. This gap may be minimized with a variety of carefully paced, sequential lessons. Sequential ideas discussed in depth, as one learning activity, may eliminate or minimize the gap. Small group instruction may be varied. There are a plethora of approaches or purposes when using small group work, including the following :

- peer mediated learning
- peer mediated teaching and instruction
- peer mediated discipline processes
- peer mediated project activities
- peer assisted learning.

In classroom management, the teacher needs to be certain that each student is responding and doing his/her fair share of required work. Respect for students and the teacher should help to optimize achievement. Respect for each other must be in the offing. Bad manners and ill conceive behavior hinders teachers in teaching and student progress in learning.

IN CLOSING

Burns (2007) wrote the following pertaining to three issues essential to teaching mathematics :

- It's important to help students make connections among mathematical ideas so they do not see these ideas as disconnected facts.
- It's important to build students' new understandings on the foundations of their prior learning.
- It's important to remember that students' correct answers, without accompanying explanations of how they reason, are not sufficient for judging mathematical understanding.

REFERENCES

The Author (Dr. M. Ediger) taught Holdeman Mennonite Children, among others, with eighth grade education being terminal, at Countryside School, rural Lehigh.

Kansas, 1955-57. From teacher observation, mathematics was prized highest by these pupils of all curriculum areas due to being very useful in farming such as in measuring and weighing of farm crops and livestock, among other practical ways.

Bandura, Albert (1977), Self Efficacy: Toward a Unifying Theory of Behavioral Change," *Psychological Review*, 84, 191-215.

Burns, Marilyn (2007), "Nine Ways to Catch Kids Up," *Educational Leadership*, 65 (3), 16.

Ediger, Marlow (2005),"Teaching Mathematics in the High School Setting," *College Student Journal*, 39 (4),711- 715.

Ediger, Marlow (2002), "The Supervisor of the School," Education, 122 (3), 602-604.

Ediger, Marlow (2007), "Learning Activities in the Curriculum," *College Student Journal*, 41 (4), 967- 969.

Ediger, Marlow, and D. Bhaskara Rao (2001), *Teaching Mathematics Successfully*. New Delhi, India: Discovery Publishing House.

Gardner, Howard (1993), *Multiple Intelligences: Theory Into Practice*. New York; Basic Books.

Piaget, Jean (1950), *The Psychology of Intelligence*. New York: Harcourt Brace Jovanovich.

Savithiri, V. (2006), Impact of Metacognitive Strategies in Enhancing Perceptual Skills among High School Students in Learning Geometry. Ph D., Alagappa University, India.

Searson, Robert, and Rita Dunn (2001), "The Learning Styles Teaching Model," *Science and Children*, 38 (5), 22-36.

Swars, Susan Lee, "Examining Perceptions of Mathematics Teaching Effectiveness Among Elementary Preservice Teachers with Differing Levels of Mathematics Teacher Efficacy," *Journal of Instructional Psychology*, 32 (2), 139-147.

Vygotsky. L. S. (1934, 1986), *Thought and Language*. Cambridge, Massachusetts: MIT Press.

3

CHAPTER

Trends in Teaching Mathematics

Mathematics teachers need to study trends in the curriculum to notice what needs to be changed/modified in teaching and learning situations. Individually or cooperatively, studying trends in mathematics instruction aids in upgrading the curriculum. This tends to minimize the gap between *what is* and *what should be* in guiding optimal achievement in learners. Which trends are salient to emphasize?

Innovation in the Mathematics Curriculum

The scope and sequence of each unit need to be carefully designed

Scope stresses *what* should be taught. The totality of knowledge, skills, and attitudinal objectives should be addressed here. Rational balance among these three kinds of objectives is important. New objectives may need to be added and a few modified or changed to meet current trends. Clarity in writing objectives is a must! Determining the scope of the mathematics curriculum emphasizes indepth understanding of what comprises a quality mathematics curriculum for learners.

Sequence stresses *when* specific facts, concepts, and generalizations are to be taught. Each new objective to be emphasized in teaching needs to be based on previous learnings acquired. Relating the new with the old provides for readiness in achievement. Subject-matter should not be taught in isolation, but as being related. This aids not only in achievement, but also in retention due to one idea triggering another. Thus, the order of mathematical experiences for pupils assists in securing more optimal attainment (Ediger, 2007a).

Metacognition is an important concept to stress in teaching

Here, the teacher guides pupils to reflect upon what has been learned. The pupil then rehearses what has been achieved as well as realizes what is left to learn. The learner, too, reflects upon that which lacks clarity. Self-diagnosis and remediation is involved. Vagueness in understanding and achieving objectives may then be corrected through teaching and learning as in the following :

- regrouping and renaming in one of the four basic operations of addition, multiplication, subtraction, or division
- negative numbers and their use
- changing fractions to decimals
- finding the per cent of a number (Ediger, 2007b).

The psychology of learning must permeate the instructional arena

This assists pupils to achieve objectives more readily and effectively. Psychological tenets and principles of learning need to be stressed in any iesson and unit of study. To do so can truly make for quality teaching and learning situations. The mathematics teacher must study and analyze diverse psychologies and try out different schools of thought in the classroom. The following are agreed upon principles of instruction :

- pupils need to be fully engaged in learning to optimize teaching and learning situations. Thus, learning activities must be interesting in order to attain objectives of instruction.

- pupils need to attach meaning to each process taught in ongoing iessons. They may become hindered in achieving if previously taught content was not understood. Readiness factors indicate a need for the learner to build upon acquired facts, concepts, and generalizations in mathematics.
- pupils need to perceive purpose in learning. Thus, the learner perceives reasons for finding the area or circumference of a circle. To show how the subject matter is used aids the pupil in sensing a need to learn. Motivation to learn is then emphasized in ongoing lessons and units of study (National Council Teachers of Mathematics, 1989).

Grouping pupils for instruction helps to individualize instruction

The mathematics teacher needs to study pupil progress carefully to notice how to group for instruction. Homogeneously grouped pupils are of similar achievement levels. Heterogeneous grouping stresses mixed achievement levels of learners. Pupils may also be grouped according to interests possessed in mathematics. The teacher then must place each pupil in the group which optimizes accomplishment. For example, the mathematics teacher groups selected pupils homogeneously since learners here are challenged by solving complex word problems. They are of similar ability levels. In an interest group, learners achieve more, here, due to like interests in doing a project such as developing a glossary on recently studied geometrical terms. Pupils are fascinated in working on most projects.

Large group instruction stresses teaching those learnings which all pupils need and achieve in this kind of setting. Small group instruction individualizes and elaborates on that discussed and presented in a large group session. Vygotsky (1978) was a strong advocate of small group or committee endeavors. He believed that learning occurred in social . situations whereby participants interact with each other. Ideas then "bounce off the minds" of individuals and learning occurs within the group discussion. Problem-solving in mathematics should work well in these kinds of situations. Criteria must be set up so that positive behavior is inherent. Rudeness and derogatory remarks hinder achievement among learners. Individualized activities, as a third kind of experience, provide opportunities for the pupil to pursue a task from the mathematics learning center which provides enrichment and purpose.

Resilience in learning is salient

Here, the pupil is able to rebound successfully from being unsuccessful. The teacher must provide activities which are on the developmental level of learners and provide for success. Success tends to motivate and activate pupils to achieve more complex ordered learnings. However, situations occur, in all of life, where a lack of success is experienced. Thus with encouragement and appropriate learning activities, the pupil is able to develop feelings of success with resilience being an end result. Resilience is a marvelous trait in which the pupil is again ready to pursue a new objective. Not giving up is important! The teacher or a peer may well be able to provide the incentive to keep working and trying. There is much to learn in the mathematics curriculum and each day presents opportunities to attain, accomplish, and master subject matter as well as needed skills (Ediger, 2008).

A positive self-concept is necessary for pupils to feel they can achieve mathematical objectives in a favorable way

Adequate background information provides readiness for tackling a new process or procedure in an ongoing lesson. An advance organizer may be used as a teaching strategy to introduce a mathematical unit which involves the teacher providing an overview of what will be studied by pupils. Concrete (objects and items), semi-concrete (illustrations, diagrams, picture charts, video tapes, dramatizations, and computerized programs), as well as abstract (mathematics basal textbooks, quality supplementary work books and work sheets, as well as computer programs), might well be used as learning activities and in teaching strategies to provide for individual differences in the classroom (Myers, 2008).

Support systems, too, help pupils to feel more positive when experiencing difficulties in attempting to achieve objectives. Thus, there is assistance from the teacher, teacher aid, and/or peers when help is needed in a given situation. The assistance is provided in a positive manner with no ridiculing or rude remarks. Then too, pupils like to hear praise for work well done. Each pupil may receive praise if his/her achievement has improved over previous performances. The self concept then provides confidence within the learner to attain more complex learnings. Pupils need to possess feelings of belonging and acceptance in the classroom, as well as have esteem needs met.

Mathematics teachers need to grow and develop in teaching skills and knowledge in a sequential manner

Through inservice education, mathematics teachers develop confidence that they can and do teach well to meet a variety of classroom needs of pupils. English Language learners (ELL), the mentally retarded, and the gifted, among others, can be assisted to achieve as optimally as possible. Inservice education may consist of workshops, faculty meetings, taking online and on campus course work, research projects, and reading recent literature on teaching mathematics from the school's professional library assists teachers to develop confidence to do a good job in teaching pupils (See Wiske, 2004).

IN CLOSING

Teachers of mathematics need to study recent trends in teaching pupils. These trends may be tried out in the classroom and modified, if need be. The important point is to provide for individual differences in the classroom and assist each pupil to optimize achievement.

REFERENCES

Ediger, Marlow (2007a), *School Science Education*. New Delhi, India: Discovery Publishing House.

Ediger, Marlow (2007b), "Readiness for Mathematics Learning and the Student," *Experiments in Education*, 35 (8), 1-5.

Ediger, Marlow (2008), "Modern School Mathematics," *College Student Journal*, 42 (4), 986-989.

Myers, Perla (2008), "Why? Why? Why? Future Teachers Discover Mathematics in Depth," *Phi Delta Kappan*, 88 (9), 696.

National Council Teachers of Mathematics (1989), *Curriculum and Evaluation Standards for School Mathematics*. Reston, Va: NCTM.

Vygotsky, Len (1978), *Mind in Society: The Development of Higher Psychological Processes*. Cambridge, Massachusetts: Harvard University Press.

Wiske, S. (2004), "Using Technology to Dig Deep for Meaning," *Educational Leadership*, 62 (1) 8.

Problems in Teaching Mathematics

The Mathematics Teacher must have thorough Knowledge and Skill in Teaching and Learning Situations

He/she must also understand the approximate developmental level of the child in order to provide a strategy which engages the learner to achieve vital objectives of instruction. Pupils differ from each other in many ways and these need to be considered in planning for instruction. For example, they reveal differences in mathematical intelligence and ability. These talents need nurturing, while other abilities, too, must be attained as optimally as possible. In a competitive society, pupils need to become proficient in mathematics for use in school and in society (Ediger, 2008).

Seven Problems in Guiding Pupil Achievement and Progress

Pupils must be challenged in ongoing learning opportunities

The objectives to be achieved need to infer high expectations from the teacher and yet each objective is attainable. Effort must be forth by the learner to develop, grow, and achieve. Encouragement needs to be in the offing. Scaffolding as a method of teaching stresses that the pupil's "proximal zone of development" makes it possible to move from where he/she is presently in achievement and then attain a selected higher ideal of accomplishment. Through teaching cues and use of appropriate materials of instruction, the pupil can achieve the otherwise too complex objective of instruction. Scaffolding then emphasizes assisting pupils from their present state of achievement to a challenging new level of attainment. That difference from what is to what is desired stresses scaffolding. The teacher's role is to ascertain where each pupil is now in achievement as compared to where the desired level at which the pupil should be. It is not easy to do this. It requires judgment, knowledge, and skill of the teacher (Vygotsky, 1978).

The mathematics teacher must provide for individual differences among learners

Thus, the math teacher needs to possess adequate knowledge of individual pupil achievement. Selected pupils will be quite independent in achievement of objectives. Others will need more assistance. In providing for individual differences in the classroom, the teacher needs to :

- achieve a wide repertoire of teaching skills
- managing mathematics classes effectively
- design a meaningful mathematics curriculum
- feel motivated to sequentially improve pupil achievement
- read articles on improving teaching and learning situations (Ediger, 2001).

Selected pupils might need help in reading word problems

The mathematics teacher needs to be a teacher of reading in order to provide help where decoding words is involved in achieving objectives. Thus, he/she may read aloud, while struggling pupils in reading follow along in their basal mathematics textbooks. In this way, pupils may be aided in understanding what has been read rather than being frustrated and hindered in comprehension. Assistance in word recognition/comprehension may also be given in the following ways :

- helping learners to use context clues
- guiding pupils to use cues such as initial consonants and their related sounds to recognize unknown words
- using picture clues to recognize an unknown word. Thus if a pupils gets stuck on a word, he/she may see if an illustration on that age gives away the unknown word
- dividing an unknown word into syllables to notice if this aids in recognizing the unknown
- looking for a smaller known word inside of the longer unknown word (Ediger, 2006).

The teacher must have a good knowledge of mathematics in order to help pupils attach meaning to what is not understood

To frequently, teachers lack indepth knowledge of mathematics to guide pupils who fail to attach meaning to what is being taught. If pupils fail to understand, the teacher must use relevant knowledge to assist pupils in goal attainment. A different algorism, a new teaching aid used such as a place value chart, a fraction chart used to teach equivalent fractions, among other vital procedures, assist pupils in achieving objectives. The math teacher needs to stay abreast of current knowledge and methodology to help pupils attain as optimally as possible (See Kennedy and Tipps, 1991).

Quality attitudes arise as a result of interacting with learning activities in the math curriculum

Strategies in teaching need to provide for success in attaining challenging objectives. The learner needs to feel he/she can and does achieve. With metacognition, the pupil reflects upon what was accomplished specifically in ongoing lessons and units of study. With reflection, the pupil reviews and rehearses. He/she also realizes gaps n knowledge and skills which need to be remedied in teaching and learning. Self diagnosis stresses that remedial work may need to be emphasized.

Good attitudes toward mathematics help in wanting to learn more subject matter. If high quality attitudes prevail, the chances are the learner will be as 2001).

Selected pupils might need help in reading word problems

The mathematics teacher needs to be a teacher of reading in order to provide help where decoding words is involved in achieving objectives. Thus, he/she may read aloud, while struggling pupils in reading follow along in their basal mathematics textbooks. In this way, pupils may be aided in understanding what has been read rather than being frustrated and hindered in comprehension. Assistance in word recognition/comprehension may also be given in the following ways :

- helping learners to use context clues
- guiding pupils to use cues such as initial consonants and their related sounds to recognize unknown words
- using picture clues to recognize an unknown word. Thus if a pupils gets stuck on a word, he/she may see if an illustration on that age gives away the unknown word
- dividing an unknown word into syllables to notice if this aids in recognizing the unknown
- looking for a smaller known word inside of the longer unknown word (Ediger, 2006).

The teacher must have a good knowledge of mathematics in order to help pupils attach meaning to what is not understood

To frequently, teachers lack indepth knowledge of mathematics to guide pupils who fail to attach meaning to what is being taught. If pupils fail to understand, the teacher must use relevant knowledge to assist pupils in goal attainment. A different algorism, a new teaching aid used such as a place value chart, a fraction chart used to teach equivalent fractions, among other vital procedures, assist pupils in achieving objectives. The math teacher needs to stay abreast of current knowledge and methodology to help pupils attain as optimally as possible (Kennedy and Tipps, 1991).

Quality attitudes arise as a result of interacting with learning activities in the math curriculum

Strategies in teaching need to provide for success in attaining challenging objectives. The learner needs to feel he/she can and does achieve. With metacognition, the pupil reflects upon what was accomplished specifically in ongoing lessons and units of study. With reflection, the pupil reviews and rehearses. He/she also realizes gaps n knowledge and skills which need to be remedied in teaching and learning. Self diagnosis stresses that remedial work may need to be emphasized.

Good attitudes toward mathematics help in wanting to learn more subject matter. If high quality attitudes prevail, the chances are the learner will be as successful as abilities permit. However, the pupil must always reach out, feel inward challenge, and compete against the self to optimize achievement (Ediger, 2006).

Continuous inservice education is a must!

Teaching becomes increasingly motivated when the teacher feels he/she is a professional in mathematics instruction. There are different ways to foster growth, development, and progress as a teacher :

- quality workshops in which participants apply in the classroom that which was presented. Participants might then provide feedback on how the innovative approach worked in teaching and learning situations.

The results are discussed, and, perhaps, result in additional innovations.

- internet courses which emphasize teaching mathematics. These online courses are given by accredited colleges and universities. Both content and methodology are being stressed.
- classes taken on accredited, higher education campuses. These provide opportunities for acquiring subject matter, as well as methods of teaching.
- attendance at local, state, and national conferences in teaching of mathematics.
- an independent study taken which involves research on teaching and learning. A variety of reference sources are used which focuses on high quality research methodology.
- seminars developed which encourage local mathematics teachers and professors discussing the implementation of recent trends in teaching.
- grade level meetings to look at innovative ideas used in teaching.
- faculty meetings involving discussing mentoring in the classroom (National Council Teachers of Mathematics, 1989).

Parent/teacher conferences are important to discuss the offspring's progress in mathematics achievement

Different facets of pupil progress need analyzing with recommendations made to facilitate learning. Parents and the school must work cooperatively to solve problems. By working together, the involved pupil should have assurance that his/her achievement does matter to significant others. A portfolio can be an excellent way for the child to communicate to the teacher and parent what has been done to achieve objectives of instruction. The learner may then pinpoint from the portfolio, for example, what has been accomplished in mathematics on selected days (Peressini, 1997).

IN CONCLUSION

Throughout the mathematics curriculum, the teacher must stress critical and creative thinking, as well as problem solving. These skills are relevant now as well as in society. They are salient in school as well as at the future work place.

REFERENCES

Ediger, Marlow (2001), *Teaching Mathematics Successfully.* New Delhi, India : Discovery Publishing House.

Ediger, Marlow (2006a), "Scaffolding and the Reading Curriculum," *Iowa Educational Leadership*, 8 (4), 24-26.

Ediger, Marlow (2006b), "Writing in the Mathematics Curriculum," *Journal of Instructional Psychology*, 33 (1),120-123.

Ediger, Marlow (2008), "Modern School Mathematics," *College Student Journal*, 42 (4),986-989.

Kennedy, Leonard M., and Steve Tipps (1991), *Guiding Children's Learning of Mathematics.* Belmont, California: Wadsworth Publishing Company.

National Council Teachers of Mathematics (1989), *Curriculum and Evaluation Standards for School Mathematics.* Reston, Virginia: NCTM.

Peressini, D. (1997), "Parental Reform of Mathematics Education," *The Mathematics Teacher*, 90 (6), 423-427.

Vygotsky, Len (1978), Mind in Society: *The Development of Higher Psychological Process.* Cambridge, Massachusetts: Harvard University Press.

5

CHAPTER

Quality Teaching in Mathematics

The best teaching possible needs to accrue in the mathematics curriculum. Pupils also need to become proficient in using mathematics in every day situations in life. Individuals buy goods and services. They pay for these in different ways, including cash. Here, persons need to be able to compute the total cost of items purchased and then pay for them using adequate currency amounts.

In the school setting, much use is made of number such as how many pupils will eat in the cafeteria at noon or how many want milk in the school milk program? There are, indeed, a plethora of situations involving the use of mathematics. What might the teacher then do to assist pupils to develop proficiency in numeracy and use mathematics effectively in school and in society?

Teaching and Learning in Mathematics

A major problem in teaching is that the teacher may wish to move forward too rapidly within a lesson which makes for pupil difficulty in keeping up with the facts, concepts, and generalizations being taught. The mathematics teacher must pace lessons whereby pupils may be successful in mastering the content presented. If the pacing is too rapid, pupils may not attach meaning to what is being taught. Toward the other end of the continuum, if the pacing is too slow, boredom may set in. The teacher must observe pupils carefully while teaching to notice if there is understanding of subject-matter being taught (Ediger and Rao, 2002).

There needs to be adequate pupil interaction with content being taught. The mathematics teacher may then be more certain that each pupil does attach meaning to ensuing content. For example, the teacher may observe pupils, at their desks, if they can show the meaning of regrouping by taking a set of fourteen sticks and placing them into a set of ten with four remaining. The resulting number may be shown in the semi-concrete, such as 14 sticks being equal to one ten and four ones on a place value chart. Numerous markers may be used to show meaning, as well as hands on approaches to learning. Active involvement of learners is better than being passive recipients, according to research findings (Ediger, 2008).

Interaction among pupils needs to be encouraged. Thus, ideas may circulate among pupils when cooperative endeavors are used in problem solving. Pupils then contribute in problem solving situations and build on the thinking of others. Ideas and contributions must be respected and politeness must be inherent in the discussion. This aids in more input from learners. A relaxed environment for cooperative endeavors encourages thinking. Vygotsky (1978) stressed the importance of small group work in which ideas "bounce of the heads" of learners. He also emphasized the concept of *scaffolding* in teaching and learning situations. Thus, if a pupil does not understand a complex concept in mathematics and yet it is achievable, The teacher may sequence with concrete and semi-concrete learning activities, in small steps, which then leads the learner to the initial complex concept in the abstract.

Learners need to develop connections in ongoing lessons and units of study. They need to learn, for example, the connectedness of $5 \times 4 = 4 \times 5$. Thus, selected structural ideas become salient such as the commutative and associative properties of multiplication and addition as well as the inverse operation of addition and subtraction, and multiplication and division. Also, pupils need to connect the mathematics curriculum with the self in solving personal problems. Then too, mathematical problems as they relate to society must find solutions. The learner does not live unto an island by the self, but is interrelated to and with others (Ediger, 2006).

Pupils need encouragement to be creative in finding their own best way to solve problems. There are different algorithms to use in finding answers to many problems. Mathematics teachers may present models here as well as support pupils who do venture out with novel ideas for solutions. Creativity is useful presently for learners as well as for the future in the societal arena. Innovations and progress have come about due to creative ideas being stressed (National Council Teachers of Mathematics, 1989).

Making estimations in terms of answers to problems is salient for pupils. It is practical to be able to make quality estimations such as in distances and in costs of items purchased. This takes knowledge and skills which are built up sequentially. In all situations in teaching mathematics, pupils need to experience interesting activities to achieve vital objectives of instruction. They need to perceive purpose or reasons for acquiring important knowledge and skills.

A rich mathematics vocabulary must be developed to perform diverse algorithms as well as to communicate mathematical ideas. The vocabulary terms must have meaning to be used effectively in contextual situations (Burns, 2007).

A professional mathematics teacher needs to posses pedagogical content knowledge and includes :

- what ideas about or understanding of a concept students are likely to have before instruction

- typical difficulties students tend to have in learning a given concept or topic
- what order to introduce concepts and skills to minimize confusion about a topic
- what strategies work to help different kinds of students overcome common difficulties
- how to choose and use instructional materials
- what models/analogies/visualizations/activities work well to convey specific understandings
- how to assess what students have learned about a given topic (Jeyanthi, 2008).

It is very important for the mathematics teacher to understand mathematical knowledge and skills possessed by pupils. A pretest and direct observation of each pupil's achievement will provide much information in terms of what the starting point should be in teaching an ensuing lesson or unit of study. From that point on, the teacher may design a curriculum based on developmental needs of pupils. Diagnosis of learning difficulties, too, must be analyzed. Remediation efforts may then follow. The mathematics teacher might well teach in a way that sequential learnings accrue. The mathematics teacher must continually observe individual pupils to notice what kinds of assistance are necessary to provide for optimal pupil achievement and progress. Sequential presentations of salient concepts and generalizations are needed to provide strategies which assist pupils to make continual progress. Inductive, deductive, multi-media, problem solving, and/or tutorials, among others, may be used to help pupils overcome difficulties and achieve (Wiske, 2004).

To teach effectively, the mathematics teacher needs to be well versed in subject matter content. He/she must explain facts, concepts, and procedures clearly and in an appropriate order. Indepth understanding needs to be developed by learners. Math teachers need to be well prepared in knowledge to be able to explain what is vague or unclear to pupils. An effective teacher foresees content problems which pupils might experience. He/she also has the indepth knowledge to ascertain which facts, concepts, and generalizations to teach so that meaningful learnings accrue to pupils. Analogies may need to be used to clarify ideas for pupils. Thus, in context, the teacher may use examples through drawings, diagrams, and illustrations to show mathematical ideas to learners. Demonstrating the use of subject matter must be in proper order, developmental appropriate, challenging, and assist in achieving successful learners. Knowledge of mathematics must not be separated from processes and procedures of teaching. The goal of integrating knowledge of mathematics with pedagogy is to assist pupils in attaining sequential objectives (Peressini, 1997).

Attitudinal Development

The teacher serves as a role model for pupils in developing a quality attitude toward mathematics. The successful teacher possesses teaching efficacy. Self-efficacy is developed by the teacher in building upon previous foundations of cumulative mathematical knowledge and skills attained as well as on successful years of teaching experience. The efficacious teacher becomes confident in teaching pupils who come from various backgrounds and persuasions. These attitudes then are passed on to pupils. A positive attitude toward mathematics and toward teaching math is salient. Pupils feel this attitude coming from the teacher and it becomes a part of the repertoire of learners in the classroom. Jeyanthi (2008) lists the following characteristics of attitude :

- attitudes are evaluative and can be presented on some continuum of favorableness
- attitudes vary in intensity and direction
- some attitudes are accompanied by or connected with a person's emotions

- attitudes are relatively durable
- attitudes are learned and can therefore be taught
- attitudes are related to behavior.

Quality attitudes in teaching mathematics then is of utmost importance. The teacher presents a role model for pupil emulation. Good attitudes can be learned by pupils. Greater achievement in mathematics is possible for all learners.

References

Ediger, Mariow (2006), "Writing in the Mathematics Curriculum," Journal of Instructional Psychology, 33 (2),120-123.

Ediger, Marlow (2008), "Modern School Mathematics," *College Student Journal*, 42 (4), 986-989.

Ediger, Marlow, and D. Bhaskara Rao (2001), *Teaching Mathematics Successfully*. New Delhi, India : Discovery Publishing House.

Burns, Marilyn (2007), "Nine Ways to Catch Kids Up," *Educational Leadership*, 65 (3),16-21.

Jeyanthi, S. (2008), Cognitive and Attitudinal Correlates of Teaching Performance of B.Ed., Mathematics Students. Ph D Mother Teresa Women's University, Kodaikanal, India. 43-44,47)

National Council Teachers of Mathematics (1989), *Curriculum and Evaluation Standards for School Mathematics*. Reston, Va.: NCTM.

Peressini, D. (1997), "Parental Reform of Mathematics Education," The Mathematics Teacher, 423-427.

Vygotsky, L. S. (1978), *Mind in Society: the Development of Higher Psychological Processes*. Cambridge, Massachusetts: Harvard University Press.

Wiske, S. (2004), "Use Technology to dig for Meaning," *Educational Leadership*, 62(1), 478.

6

CHAPTER

Direct Teaching vs Constructivism in Mathematics

Direct teaching may be placed on one end of the continuum whereas constructivism toward the other end when stressing a formal versus an informal approach of mathematics instruction. There can be a plethora of in between points. Which methods are generally superior in teaching mathematics? Direct teaching usually stresses information moving from the teacher to students whereas in constructivism, the learner develops knowledge in an informal method of teaching. In either case, it does take well prepared teachers with a strong mathematics background. Each approach also requirers math teachers highly knowledgeable about methods of instruction. Adequate materials of instruction must be available to provide for individual student differences in achievement. Class size, too, needs to be such that the mathematics teacher may provide assistance to learners as necessary.

Direct Teaching of Mathematics

With direct teaching, the mathematics teacher may design the curriculum in terms of choosing relevant objectives for pupils to attain. These are in three categories. The first being knowledge objectives. Here, the math teacher needs to evaluate the worth of each chosen knowledge end. Vital facts, concepts, and generalizations need to be emphasized in teaching. Second, skills objectives need to be selected by the teacher. Skills stress putting the knowledge to use. Using what has been acquired is salient. Knowledge is retained longer if application is emphasized. Objectives need to be stated in measurable terms. It can then be determined if a pupil has/has not been successful in goal attainment. The third category to be designed into the math curriculum is attitudinal objectives. With quality attitudes, the chances are the pupil will have a greater desire to learn in mathematics (Ediger and Rao, 2003).

With direct teaching, the mathematics teacher observes pupils carefully to notice if they understand what is taught. He/she adapts the speed of teaching to pupil needs. With quality university preparation for math teaching, the teacher may expound on details of a mathematical operation which is necessary for pupil understanding of subject matter taught. The teacher may proceed as directly as possible with teaching a new concept or process. Carefully selected basal mathematics textbooks provides the basis for choosing learning activities for pupils. How specific each sequential step of teaching is depends upon the needs of pupils. Workbooks and work sheets provide additional and remedial learnings where needed. Pupils need to understand the inward meaning of any operation on number. Thus to understand division of fractions, the pupil in a meaningful way must attach meaning as to why the divisor is inverted, followed by multiplication of numerator times numerator as well as denominator times denominator with the product of the numerators placed over the products of the denominator. The sequence of activities involved in teaching need to be broken down into manageable parts to assist pupil understanding and clarification. Concrete, semi-concrete, and abstract materials of instruction need to be used. Valid and reliable tests may then be used to appraise pupil achievement. Direct teaching is a learning style of selected pupils (Searson and Dunn, 2001).

Direct teaching emphasizes a subject-centred curriculum. Important mathematical ideas need to be identified and taught. There are essential facts, concepts, and generalizations which pupils must attain to be successful in school presently as well as in future society. These ideas need identification and must be taught. Accountability for their achievement by pupils rests with schools. Testing is a major way to ascertain if pupils have successfully mastered essential content. State and district administered tests, with high validity and reliability, might well reveal how well pupils are progressing. Tests may also be used to diagnose individual learner progress in mathematics. Remediation methods of teaching may follow (Guild, 1997).

Constructivism in Teaching Mathematics

Teachers who follow constructivism as a psychology of learning believe that each pupil constructs his/her own knowledge. Lecture is not an appropriate way of helping pupils to achieve. Rather, the math teacher provides learning activities whereby pupils sequence their own learnings. The following situations then accrue :

- pupils are encouraged to raise questions pertaining to ensuing facts, concepts, and generalizations being studied.
- questions pertaining to what is not understood might well be answered with another question or series of questions which assists the pupil to ascertain his/her own answers.
- power resides within the student when having control over his/her own learning, such as suggesting possible topics to study or pursing personal problems to solve in mathematics.

- math teachers become facilitators and guides when assisting the learning process. Instead of direct teaching, they help pupils with encouragement and needed information to pursue within the framework of ongoing lessons and units of study.
- peers may be actively involved in solving assigned math problems.

Cooperative learning, recommended by Vygotsky (1978), advocated that ideas "bounce off the minds" of participants during a discussion, thus leading to *scaffolding* in learning. With scaffolding, An achievable complex mathematical concept may not be understood, but with a sequence of activities becomes meaningful and leads to understanding the initial difficult idea. The activities might well involve continuing discussions in a session leading to meaningful learnings.

With constructivism, pupils construct knowledge rather than receiving it passively. Interaction with mathematical content is important as well as with the physical and social environment. Pupils tend to look for meaning and order in mathematics achievement. Lecturing as a method of teaching does not provide situations for constructing ideas and tends to minimize learner's understanding subject matter content. The *zone of proximal development* (Vygotsky, 1978) emphasizes the importance of pupils reaching toward higher levels of accomplishment. It stresses where a pupil is presently in achievement as compared to where he/she might achieve successfully. The gap represents what may be eliminated with sequential learnings in a thinking situation, such as peers challenging each other in cooperative learning.

Pupils gain confidence in successfully exploring increasingly complex ideas in mathematics. The teacher monitors and may serve as a coach. Active learning in social situations is emphasized. Pupils accept responsibility for learning as they gain confidence in the self. The self-concept is salient here. Supportive teachers and peers assist in developing feelings of motivation. First hand experiences, not lecture, aid in establishing meaning in ongoing learning experiences. Good attitudes are then emphasized toward mathematics, other learners, and the school (NCTM, 1989).

Constructivism emphasizes quality group dynamics with interaction among the teacher, pupil, and task. Committee and small group work involves all participating and no one dominating. Ideas flow within and among members and not between a few pupils only. Respect and caring is shown toward each participant. This aids in pupils learning by discovery within the framework of life like mathematical problems. Learning by discovery fascinates pupils and fosters interest in discoveries made. Critical and creative thinking used in problem solving experiences makes for skills useful in school and in society. Challenging, but achievable learnings, need to be in the offing. The pupil owns the problem and needs to monitor his/her own progress. Assistance, support, and guidance are available when pupils work on mathematical problems and specific difficulties are faced. The assistance comes from a variety of sources including teachers and peers (Peressini, 2006).

CONCLUSION

In summary, Brown (2003) lists conditions for a curriculum which helps to ensure student success in learning and includes the following :

- Classrooms must be learner-centered, not content centered.
- Teachers must believe that all students can learn.
- Learner centered classrooms must be success oriented.
- Learning must be active, not passive.
- Instruction must be developmental appropriate.
- Instruction must address many different leaning styles.
- Students must be allowed to work together.

- Teachers must be facilitators of learning, not just presenters of content.
- Teachers must provide students with choices.
- Learning must be contextually relevant.
- Many different forms of assessment must be employed.
- Teaches must be reflective practitioners.

REFERENCES

Brown, David (2003), "A Learner Centered Curriculum Based on Award Winning Literature," *Education*, 124 (1), 76-85.

Ediger, Marlow (2003), *Teaching Mathematics Successfully*. New Delhi, India : Discovery Publishing House.

Guild, P. B. (1997), "Where do the Learning Theories Overlap?" *Educational Leadership* 55, 30-31.

National Council Teachers of Mathematics (1989), Curriculum and Evaluation Standards for School Mathematics. Reston, Virginia: NCTM.

Peressini, D. (2006), "Parental Reform of Mathematics Education," *The Mathematics Teacher*, 90 (6), 423-427.

Searson, Robert, and Rita Dunn (2001), "The Learning Style Teaching Model," *Science and Children*, 38 (5), 22-36.

Vygotsky, L. S. (1978), *Mind In Society: The Development of Higher Psychological Processes*. Cambridge, Massachusetts: Harvard University Press.

7

CHAPTER

Substitute Teacher and Mathematics Curriculum

Too frequently, the complaint has been that substitute teachers merely baby sit and do not actually teach students. Thus, the feeling may persist that substitute teachers do not need to be prepared for their presence in the classroom. The authors believe that substitute teachers need to be well prepared for each day of teaching and quality sequence in student learning is being emphasized. Student achievement needs to move forward as sequentially as possible. Well prepared and motivated substitute teachers must be in the offing. This paper will pertain to helping these teachers to grow, develop, and achieve.

Inservice Education and the Substitute Teacher

School districts need to provide quality inservice education for substitute teachers at the beginning of a new school year. This should make it possible for assisting learners to benefit fully from each day of teaching. The mathematics curriculum needs to stress meaningful learnings for students. Thus, the substitute teacher needs to assist young children to count, add, and subtract with the use of markers. Thus, children learn to count as they point sequentially to each marker. This makes it possible for young learners to show a set of three, for example, when using these markers. They may combine markers to show addition, e.g., two markers and one marker. The concrete representation may be shown in the abstract : 2 + 1 = 3. When ready, these students may attach meaning to subtraction-three markers minus one marker equals two markers. The inverse operation of subtraction is then shown meaningfully. These foundational concepts assist students to build upon previously understood subject matter. Inductive and deductive learning may be stressed (Ediger and Rao, 2003).

Demonstration teaching should help the substitute teacher in teaching students in the classroom. It provide models to emulate in a classroom. The substitute teacher needs to show in an interesting way place value learnings to students. A neatly developed place value chart may be constructed with the names of place holders such as ones, tens, hundreds, etc. listed at the top with pockets underneath to hold congruent . paper strips (manipulative materials). Thus, for example, to show the numeral 312 in the place value chart, two slips of paper may be put into the ones pocket, one in the tens, and three in the hundreds pocket. To add 134 to 312, four congruent slips may be put into the ones pocket, and three to the tens pocket with one to the tens column. The student may then be guided to perceive meaningfully that 312 + 134 = 446. The inverse operation may be indicated in subtracting 312 from 446 by manipulating slips of paper from the ones, tens, and hundreds columns. All four operations—addition, subtraction, multiplication and division-may be shown on the place value chart, using the congruent slips of paper and the related abstract numerals. When the place value chart is no longer needed, students may work with the abstract numerals only. With proper sequence in the mathematics curriculum, students should be able to achieve subject matter content in moving from the concrete (markers) to the semi-concrete (place value chart), to the abstract. Students must be actively involved in using the manipulative materials to show operations on number. An indepth understanding of base ten numeration is important for all learners. Interest in learning is a powerful factor in achievement. A variety of activities and methods of instruction need to be used including computer based instruction (Ediger, 2006).

Objectives for student attainment should include number words and mathematical symbols applicable to operation on numbers. Readiness needs to be in evidence so that students may benefit from ensuing lessons. Hurrying through different lessons is not a goal, but attaching meaning to each sequential step of learning is salient. Thus in geometry lessons and units of study, students must understand subsequent learnings pertaining to points, lines, rays, and line segments in space figures, and thus experience ordered success. Among others, learnings in congruent and similar geometric figures should become a definite part of the student's mathematical vocabulary (Noddings, 2008).

With inservice education, the substitute teacher needs to perceive models to use in quality teaching and learning situations. Practical situations should also be used in mathematics instruction. Thus a student may have, for example, Rs. 60.35 and needs Rs. 83.59 to buy a baseball glove, how much more needs to be earned. The place value chart may be used here. Or, if the student is ready, the abstract phase of learning might well be used in determining how much more money is necessary to buy the baseball glove. Sometimes, the practical phase of learning is highly motivating to students. During the 1955-57 school year, the first author taught in a two teacher rural school near Lehigh, Kansas. There were six Holdeman Mennonite children in the classroom. Eighth grade is terminal education. The students did much better in mathematics than social studies or other subject-matter areas, due to their perceiving the utilitarian value of arithmetic. Mathematics textbooks were then more rural orientated with word problems on how many bushels would go into a metal grain bin with the dimensions of the bin given. Students learned about how many pounds in a bushel of wheat, oats, and corn. This is common knowledge to the writer who grew up on a farm, but to his professional colleagues at a university, this knowledge was basically unknown. Culture, time, and place assist in determining what is relevant (Savithiri, 2006).

Problems may always be grafted to meet practical needs of students in mathematics in diverse cultures. This merely says to adapt course work to fall within the experiences of learners. The creative substitute teacher needs to think of a variety of rich experiences for children. The NCTM Standards that pertain to early mathematics experiences for Kindergarten through grade four emphasize the following :

Standard 6: Number Sense and Numeration, the mathematics curriculum should include whole number concepts and skills so that students can :

- construct number meanings through real world experiences and the use of physical materials
- develop number sense
- interpret the multiple uses of numbers encountered in the real world (National Council Teachers of Mathematics, 1989).

Inservice Education for Substitute Teachers

A well prepared substitute teacher experiences quality opportunities for growth and professionalism. What is presented in inservice education needs to be functional and based upon the best in research practices. These programmes must present learning activities involving master teachers showing how to make mathematical learnings meaningful, interesting, and purposeful. A hands on approach needs to be used. Substitute teachers need ample opportunities to try out concepts and generalizations in a contextual classroom setting. These learnings may include the following in inservice education :

- regrouping in addition, subtraction, multiplication, and division
- problem solving and project methods of instruction
- diverse algorithms and computational methods
- the four operations on fractions and making sense of mixed numbers, as well as renaming and reducing fractions to their lowest terms
- extending understanding of fractions to the use of decimals and per cents
- evaluation of learner progress and reporting student progress to parents (Ediger, 2007).

Substitute teachers need to be well-educated to assist students to do well in the mathematics curriculum. They must be able to guide each learner to make continuous progress in knowledge, skills, and attitudes.

IN CLOSING

Students need to be able to monitor their very own progress. The substitute teacher then must assist each student to reflect upon his/her progress. By reflecting, the learner thinks about what was understood and what needs more work be it in mathematical facts, concepts, and/or generalizations. Also by reflecting, the student may think of new ways to use mathematics in every day life.

REFERENCES

Ediger, Marlovv (2006), "Writing in the Mathematics Curriculum," *Journal of Instructional Psychology*, 33 (1), 120-123.

Ediger, Marlow (2007), "Teacher Observation to Assess Student Achievement," *Journal of Instructional Psychology*, 34 (3), 137-139.

Ediger, Marlow, and D. Bhaskara Rao (2000), *Teaching Mathematics Successfully*. New Delhi, India: Discovery Publishing House.

National Council Teachers of Mathematics (1989), *Curriculum and Evaluation Standards for School Mathematics*. Reston, Va : NCTM, 38.

Noddings, Nel (2008), "All Our Students Thinking," *Educational Leadership 65*, (5), 8-13.

Savithiri, V. (2006), Impact of Metacognitive Strategies in Enhancing Perceptual Skills Among High School Students on Learning Geometry. Ph D theses evaluated by the writer for Alagappa University, Karaikudi, India.

8 CHAPTER

Mathematics Curriculum and Psychology of Learning

How might the mathematics teacher optimize pupil achievement in mathematics? This is a continual question for any professional. What may assist pupils to focus more on the objectives being stressed in mathematics? Mathematics is one of the basics in the curriculum and needs quality teaching and learning procedures.

Teaching in a Pupil Centred Mathematics Programme

Mathematics teachers must meet salient needs of pupils in ongoing lessons and units of study. Which principles of learning will assist in guiding optimal pupil achievement? First, teachers need to provide adequate background experiences in order for pupils to benefit from the ensuing lesson. Thus, pupils need to achieve necessary knowledge and skills related to new learning opportunities to be presented. If pupils then are to learn about borrowing in subtraction, do they possess needed concepts and generalizations pertaining to place value? If the answer is in the negative, the mathematics teacher must assist pupils to understand place value by using the needed materials such as place value charts and manipulative objects.

This activity should lead to success in learning about borrowing in subtraction (Ediger and Rao, 2003).

Second, teachers need to provide quality sequence in pupil learning. Covering subject-matter too rapidly may make for too many pupils left behind in achieving. Good sequence stresses challenging learning opportunities for pupils and yet success in achievement is an end result. Success generally is a motivator to involved pupils to tackle new learnings. With quality sequence, pupils perceive relationships in ideas, and not focus upon isolated subject matter. If, for example, addition and subtraction are viewed in isolation from each other, it takes longer for pupils to acquire new ideas being presented in ongoing lessons. However, if subtraction is perceived as the inverse operation of addition, pupils will progress sooner to increasingly more complex learnings. Clarity of ideas in these relationships may be shown with markers to indicate addition and then subtraction (Ediger, 2007).

Third, teachers need to be certain that pupils attach meaning to what is being taught. This means that learners must understand what is in the objective being emphasized. For example, if pupils are studying congruent geometric figures, they need to demonstrate from the ongoing lesson that they can explain and show congruency. Being able to do these things will provide feedback to the teacher as to what is understood. Pupils always need to understand the present objective before they are taught more complex ideas. If they do not understand, this will be shown in future learnings being pursued. Meaning attached to concepts and generalizations taught makes for increased retention. Retained learnings may then be used to provide readiness for the ensuing lesson. Success in learning is then more likely to accrue (Sridevi, 2007).

Fourth, mathematics teachers need to emphasize purpose in having pupils achieve new ideas pertaining to the subject matter to be presented. Having pupils perceive reasons for attaining new objectives in the ongoing lesson in mathematics, assists in accepting the goals being stressed. There should be reasons for having pupils, for example, finding the area of a square or rectangle. Practical situations abound such as finding the area of a classroom for putting in a new carpet or installing it in a home setting. Flexible thinking by the teacher in developing purposeful, practical learning situations helps pupils to perceive purpose for achieving. It also facilitates motivation to learn.

Fifth, higher order thinking skills (HOTS) must be stressed, particularly when pupils work on word problems. These problems may come from the basal textbook or be teacher designed. As a university supervisor of student teachers in the public schools, the writer observed selected fifth and sixth grade pupils write clearly worded story problems, challenging for others to solve. Creative thinking was definitely in evidence. Student teachers and cooperating teachers wrote some excellent, realistic story problems which supplemented the basal textbook. Critical thinking was necessary to find needed answers. Here, pupils separated necessary information from that which was not needed to solve problems (Ediger and Rao, 2006).

Sixth, inductive learning must be a salient objective in the mathematics curriculum. Learning by discovery then becomes important in teaching and learning. There are selected approaches which might be used to implement a strategy for pupil inductive learning. Learners do need appropriate background information in order to learn inductively, but not to the point whereby the activity will be routine. There is excitement in learning by discovery. Pupils need opportunities to hypothesize and try out educated guesses on solving a new process in mathematics. For example, pupils may offer solutions on how to solve a new type of word problem involving three steps. The word problem is written on the chalkboard or presented in a duplicated paper. In either case, a small number of pupils (four or five) should be on a committee so that more frequent participation is possible as compared to the class as a whole. As pupils interact with each other in an atmosphere of respect, brain storming is being stressed. Duplication of ideas may not be emphasized unless this is needed for problem solution. Pupils find this activity to be exciting and interesting. It does make pupils do indepth thinking to offer solutions. The mathematics teacher may need to offer some clues along the way to keep the activity moving forward. Clues given should be as limited as possible. The writer has noticed several of these highly successful learning by discovery activities when supervising university student teachers (Ediger, 2005).

Mathematics is the most exact science and its conclusions are capable of exact proof. All mathematics truths are relative and conditional. Mathematics may be regarded either as a body of achievements or as an intellectual enterprise. Mathematics draws its main strength from the following features:

1. abstractness,
2. generalization,
3. logical consistency,
4. depth,
5. precision,
6. seriousness,
7. elegance,
8. economy of thought,
9. thoroughness,
10. significance,
11. clarity, and
12. permanence (Savithiri, 2006).

The above-enumerated items might well provide objectives of instruction such as in # 1 above—abstractness. There are indeed a plethora of abstract symbols such as the written/typed numerals, symbols used for operations on number, algebraic formulas for determining perimeter and area of geometrical figures, as well as lines, points, rays, among others. These learnings provide activities and opportunities for vocabulary development. Reading in mathematics, also, has its abstractness from which pupils need to perceive meaning. Also, #2 above stresses pupils developing generalizations from subject matter acquired in mathematics including the commutative/associative properties of addition and multiplication as well as the inverse operations of subtraction and division.

Metacognition Needs to be Stressed in Mathematics

Metacognition emphasizes that pupils think about thinking. It is a highly relevant tool of instruction. Mathematics with its emphasis upon logical thinking, as well as creative thought involved in problem solving must stress a developmentally appropriate set of metacognitive strategies. It is very important for pupils to think about how they added, subtracted, multiplied, and divided a given of numerals. When doing this, the learner rehearses strategies which were successful and those which were not appropriate to use. When engaged in problem solving, the pupil thinks about useful versus non-useful strategies and how the ensuing problem may be solved. Rote learning is not involved when thinking about thinking, but indepth analysis is in evidence. Intensive thought prevails.

Monitoring one's own progress is involved in metacognition. When reading mathematical subject-matter, the pupil monitors achievement in ascertaining if he/she is comprehending needed content or merely pronouncing words. Understanding what has been read requires careful monitoring. The pupil may also monitor if he/she is reading at higher levels of cognition, rather than the recall level only or largely. Additional items in monitoring reading of mathematical content emphasizes the following :

- techniques to use in identifying unknown words including phonics, syllabication, and the use of context clues. Readiness factors are salient in being able to recognize new words which comes from maturation and previous rich experiences.
- making predictions pertaining to what the ensuing selection will be about. This is done by viewing the related illustrations in the basal textbook as well as in the library book. Good predictions assist in comprehension of subject matter to be read.
- knowledge of semantics helps pupils to attach meaning to what is being read. There may be several meanings possible for sentences read and these need to be

contextually clarified. Semantics guide pupils to read subject matter meaningfully (Griffin, 2004).

Guiding Pupils' Mathematics Learnings

Mathematics teachers need to monitor their own teaching to notice what pupils need to achieve objectives successfully. Very frequently, entry behaviors of pupils is inadequate to benefit fully from instruction. A lack of quality entry behaviours will show up in not understanding an ensuing process being stressed. Readiness for the new leanings was then not in evidence. Teachers need to evaluate if pupils individually possess the necessary facts, concepts, and generalizations to benefit from ongoing instruction. Planning for teaching a new lesson should incorporate which prerequisites are needed. Thus, a new objective of instruction must be analyzed to determine which knowledge and skills are to be taught so that the learner understands the new learnings. If pupils have made certain computational errors, these need to be re-taught. Diagnosis, as to why these errors in computation occurred, must be made.

Vocabulary development in mathematics is very important. Pupils must understand thoroughly the vocabulary necessary to do good work in mathematics. Prekindergarden to grade twelve, vocabulary development needs to receive proper emphasis. Failure to achieve an objective might well be a lack of vocabulary development. For each lesson taught, the teacher needs to be certain that pupils attach meaning to the contextual meaning of words.

Pupils sometimes do not compute effectively due to a lack of meaning attached to what is being emphasized in teaching and learning situations. Knowing and understanding the meaning of basic addition, subtraction, multiplication, and division facts provides foundation learnings for increasingly complex computation skills. Among other things, they also provide foundational learnings for solving word problems correctly. Learners need to understand prerequisites for ensuing sequential abstract ideas. Possessing necessary entry behaviors is a must for achieving new objectives of instruction.

Mathematics teachers need to realize that all learning activities are developmentally appropriate for pupils. Forcing pupils to achieve an objective in mathematics for which he/she is not ready is unproductive. Objectives need to be realistic and pupils have reasonable expectations of achieving them. Jean Piaget (1950) who studied pupil behavior for over 50 years and in his research came up with different maturational stages which pupils go through. His research indicated that maturation is a key factor in learning and that children go through different stages as in the following :

- sensori-motor in which the use of the muscles and physical interaction with objects predominate. This stage lasts from birth to eighteen months/two years.
- preoperational stage (ages two to seven) whereby the child perceives one variable only, in physical objectives. The one variable may be length only or width only of objects and items perceived.
- stage of concrete operations, ages seven to eleven, in which the learner perceives several dimensions in concrete objects (length, width, and height) and is able to learn from the abstract as well as from the physical items being discussed.
- stage of abstract thought whereby the learner can now discuss ideas in the abstract without reference to real objects and items.

The above research of Piaget has salient implications for mathematics teachers. Pupils then may not have matured adequately to benefit from the ensuing lesson taught. There are stages of maturation which pupils go through in life which determines what can be achieved and learned. If learnings are too complex, failure to achieve will be in evidence. Maturation is related to the age level of the child. Hurrying in teaching with stress placed upon covering much subject matter is defeating. What matters is that pupils are ready maturation wise to benefit from the ensuing lesson taught.

Vygotsky (1934, 1986), Russian psychologist, in his studies came up with the concept of scaffolding in assisting learner progress. He advocated the zone of proximal development in viewing what should be taught to pupils. The zone dealt with a gap between what a pupil knows presently and what is to be acquired in the new learning. This gap, if reasonable, may be filled with sequential subject matter, requiring ordered content. Thus, the gap may be too wide, but, if reasonable, may be narrowed by ordering learning experiences. Scaffolding then emphasizes viewing what has been learned with what is desired, and if reasonable, the difference may be minimized with good teaching.

References

Ediger, Marlow (2005), "Teaching Mathematics in the Hight School Setting," *College Student Journal*, 39 (4), 711-715.

Ediger, Marlow (2007), "Learning Activities in the Curriculum," *College Student Journal*, 41 (4), 967-969.

Ediger, Marlow, and D. Bhaskara Rao (2003), *Teaching Mathematics Successfully*. New Delhi, India: Discovery Publishing House.

Ediger, Marlow, and D. Bhaskara Rao (2006), *Quality School Education*. New Delhi, India: Discovery Publishing House.

Griffin, Sharon (2004), "Teaching Number Sense," *Educational Leadership*, 61 (5), 39-42.

Piaget, Jean (1950), *The Psychology of Intelligence*. New York: Harcourt Brace Jovanovich.

Savithiri, V. (2006), Impact of Metacognition Strategies in Enhancing Perceptual Skills Among High School Students on Learning Geometry. Ph.D., Alagappa University, Alagappa, India.

Sredevi, K. V. (2007), "Constructivism : A Shift in the Teaching-Learning Process." *Edutracks*, 7 (4), 9-13.

Vygotsky, L. S. (1934, 1986), *Thought and Language*. Cambridge, Massachusetts: the MIT Press.

9

CHAPTER

Quality in Mathematics Curriculum

More demands are made on mathematics teachers than ever before. With mandated testing, public school students are to measure up to certain standards to be promoted to the next grade level in grades three through eight, as well as pass an exit test in high school to receive a diploma. Passing results on tests are required in mathematics, reading, and science. Mathematics has had a long history of being known as one of the basics in the curriculum.

Mathematics teachers need to prepare daily lessons involving the best objectives, learning activities, and assessment approaches. How might the mathematics teacher continue to achieve, develop, and grow in his/her professional activities? There are definite characteristics and traits of students which need attention in teaching and learning situations. These must be considered when teaching mathematics in the school setting in order to make provision for individual differences among students (Ediger, 2006).

Providing for Individual Differences in Mathematics

Students differ from each other in a plethora of ways and this must be emphasized in teaching and learning situations.

A first difference pertains to methods used in teaching. There are students who prefer clear sequential explanations, generally using a variety of instructional materials, in solving problems in mathematics. Thus, the teacher needs to possess a good grasp of mathematical facts, concepts, and generalizations to explain ideas accurately and meaningfully. The teacher secures feedback from learners to ascertain how well each is doing in the followup. Thus, students, for example, may work exercises in a workbook, from teacher devised work sheets, and from the basal textbook, among others, to reveal what was achieved. Diagnosis and reteaching might be necessary to correct misunderstandings. A pleasant voice with appropriate stress, pitch, and voice inflection assists students to achieve well. Time on task is important to develop and maintain student sequential progress in ongoing mathematics lessons and units of study (Ediger and Rao, 2002).

Somewhat toward the other end of the continuum, A mathematics teacher uses more open ended procedures of instruction. The teacher provides readiness for students in discussing practical situations involving the ensuing lesson. Illustrations help clarify what is utilitarian. Questions and comments by students are encouraged. These assist students to perceive purpose in learning. If students for example, are to find the areas of selected squares and rectangles, they are shown objects where these measurements are needed to find area. Students may choose three of the objects, as a minimum, to determine the length and width of squares and rectangles written on the chalkboard. Students may be actively involved in evaluating the previous experiences. The appraisal consists of assessing the accuracy of understanding the concepts of finding area of squares and rectangles, as well as of computations made. Emphasis is placed upon students attaching meaning to the total experience. Teacher observation, too, is used continuously in noticing the accuracy of student work on the involved tasks. Recorded anecdotal statements assist in noticing which specifics need to be stressed in the next lesson (Ediger, 2007).

Second, all students need to be accepted as persons having intrinsic worth. Teacher A is rather formal in methods of instruction. He/she stresses meeting developmental needs of students. This is done by the teacher when observing what students need sequentially in ongoing lessons in mathematics. Decisions are made by the teacher when planning each lesson carefully. Quality ordered objectives, learning activities to achieve the objectives, and evaluation procedures are implemented by the mathematics teacher. Observing and seeing that each student is following carefully what is contained in the lesson plan are musts! Patiently, re-explaining what is necessary is ongoing. A very business like atmosphere prevails in the classroom (Ediger, 2006).

Teacher B is somewhat informal in working with students. He/she also plans each lesson carefully. However, students feel free to raise queries about related topics in mathematics if these arise. Thus, for example, if a learner asks about how much more money is needed to buy a baseball glove if the amount of money on hand is given, presents opportunities for learner input. Practical applications of arithmetic might then be emphasized in the relaxed learning environment. There are times when the teacher laughs with students when humorous occasions arise. Cooperative learning is involved in problem solving experiences. Individual endeavors are also stressed to provide for different styles of learning. These problems, among others, may come from the basal textbook, from the work book, and teacher devised learning experiences. Students themselves and the teacher monitor if learners are actively engaged in working together to solve these problems (National Council Teachers of Mathematics, 1989).

Additional considerations in teaching mathematics include being positive in working with students. Thus, students should not be labeled. When supervising university student teachers in the public schools, the writer observed teachers sometimes attached labels to different ability levels. The highest achievers then were in Group A, followed by Group

Statewide tests tend to be standardized in that a commercial company developed the items for testing purposes, generally multiple choice in nature. The tests are standardized in that they contain the same content, the same directions for test taking, and the same time limits for that age level of pupils talking the test. To standardize the mathematics test, pilot studies were run to a random sample of pupils. The results were then categorized into norms for the standardized test. A pupil's results from presently taking the test are then compared to the norm group in order to secure percentile, and/or grade and age level equivalent information (Newton, 2007).

The Manual of the standardized test indicates how the test items were validated. Any standardized test must be valid. Thus, if the involved math teacher wishes to measure pupil achievement in the basic four operations on number of addition, subtraction, multiplication, and division, then the standardized test must measure pupils achievement in these four operations to be valid. They will be written for a specific age or grade level. Reliability, also, is salient in that a standardized test must measure consistently. Thus if a fourth grader receives a test result of being on the fortieth percentile, he/she should receive approximately the fortieth percentile on the second time the test is taken. This is test/retest reliability. If pupils are tested once, the odd numbered versus the even numbered test items should produce similar results for many pupils, in order for the test to be reliable. This method can be used with teacher written classroom tests since one testing usually occurs pertaining to a math test taken by pupils in the classroom. Alternate forms information reliability also may be shown in the Manual of the test being taken (National Council Teachers of Mathematics, 1989).

Most standardized test items contain multiple choice test items and this type may also be used by the teacher when he/she writes a math test. Teacher written math tests are very valuable because they may be taken by pupils throughout the school year whereas standardized tests are generally given once a year. Highly valid tests may be written covering what has been taught in a math unit of study. Thus whatever has been taught and is vital may be included in a math test. Face validity is then used. Multiple choice test items in math need to :

- possess four distractors that are plausible. If three alone are plausible, more chances for guessing the correct response occur.
- distractors should be of equivalent length so that no clues are given for the correct answer.
- correct responses should alternate among the different multiple choice test items so that no patterns are seen as to correct answers.
- have stems which are'grammatically correct with each distractor (Ediger, 2007).

Results from pupils' tests provide feedback to both learners and teachers in terms of what needs more emphasis in the mathematics curriculum. True/false test items, clearly written, have merit if the pupil needs to correct the incorrect part. This avoids the fifty percent chance of guessing an answer correctly.

Essay tests may do a good job of evaluating achievement in mathematics if the questions are :

- valid and reliable. Use of quality rubrics increases judging pupil's responses more reliably
- delimited and stress problem solving, not rote learning
- written in emphasizing higher levels of cognition such as critical and creative thinking (Ediger, 2006).

Test results then provide information for making lesson and unit decisions in teaching mathematics. Feedback to both pupils and teachers should aid in providing quality objectives, learning opportunities, and appraisal procedures in teaching mathematics.

reading professional materials in mathematical instruction, as well as in conversing with and observing quality teaching and learning situations. Improved instruction should be an end result.

References

Dymock, Susan (2007), "Comprehension Strategy Instruction : Teaching Narrative Text Structure Awareness," *The Reading Teacher*, 61 (2), 161-167.

Ediger, Marlow (2002), "The Supervisor of the School," *Education*, 122 (3), 602-604.

Ediger, Marlow (2006), "Writing in the Mathematics Curriculum," *Journal of Instructional Psychology, 2006*, (33), 120-123.

Ediger, Marlow (2007), "Learning Activities in the Curriculum," *College Student Journal*, 41 (4), 967-969.

Ediger, Marlow, and D. Bhaskara Rao (2002), *Teaching Mathematics Successfully*. New Delhi, India : Discovery Publishing House.

Eisner, Elliot (2006), "The Satisfactions of Teaching," *Educational Leadership*, 63 (6), 44-47.

Maslow, A. H. (1954), *Motivation and Personality*. New York : Harper and Row.

National Council Teachers of Mathematics (1989), *Curriculum Evaluation Standards for School Mathematics*. Reston, Virginia: NCTM.

10

CHAPTER

Data Driven Decision-making in Mathematics

Of all academic areas in the curriculum, data driven decision making works best in mathematics due to its preciseness and patterns possessed. In data driven instruction, the mathematics teacher needs to develop specific objectives which leaves little/no leeway for interpretation. The teacher teaches so that pupils attain these objectives with learning activities which possess :

- purpose or logical reasons for their use
- interest which propels learners to achieve goals
- meaning so that pupils understand indepth what is taught (Ediger, 1989).

After instruction, the math teacher may measure if pupils have achieved these objectives. Those not achieved by learners provide ensuing objectives and learning opportunities for goal attainment. There are diverse mathematics tests which may be used to document pupil progress.

Testing to Notice Achievement

Mandated mathematics tests have become exceedingly important in society. These may be state or district wide tests.

B being middle achievers, and Group C at the lowest level in homogeneous grouping for instruction. Rather, each student has much intrinsic worth and needs periodic praise for doing better than formerly in mathematics regardless of ability levels. The self concept of the student is important to consider in teaching and learning situations. He/she needs to develop feelings of "I can achieve in mathematics". Thus, self efficacy becomes salient. Here, the learner has confidence that the highest achievement is possible individually. Continuous progress is a must. Based on past experiences of being successful, quality attitudes toward mathematics is developed. Respect for each person is being emphasized. Ridicule, rudeness, and belittling should not exist in the classroom/ school environment. Harassment in any form is not conducive to student growth, development, and progress. They are a hindrance to making progress in mathematics be it for the giver or the receiver of the negative comments (Maslow, 1954).

Student individual learning styles need recognition and provided for. Selected students then learn best through inductive procedures. They prefer to find out on their own when a new process in mathematics is being stressed. The teacher facilitates learning by assisting the learner to make relevant discoveries. Instead of telling the learner how to do a new process, the teacher guides achievement here with important questions resulting in the student finding answers to his/her own queries. Others in the classroom may prefer a deductive procedure where by the mathematics teacher provides meaningful methods of arriving at solutions to queries. Thus, the student is told how to do a problem in an ordered way. The oral communication moves from teacher to the student (Eisner, 2006)

Generally, a combination of both procedures will be used. In either approach, inductive or deductive, the student needs to *reflect* upon the steps involved in having completed satisfactorily what was not understood previously. Reflecting helps the student to review and refine methods and procedures used. It also assists the student to assess the kinds of errors made and rectify what needs changing.

Students learning to monitor their individual achievement is important. Thus, for example, when reading a story problem in mathematics, the learner must notice if he/she secures main ideas necessary for problem solution. There are students who might even read well, but pay little attention to attach meanings to what was read. Learning to monitor one's own progress assists in noticing if salient subject-matter is being acquired. At a very young age, on the appropriate developmental level, students need to recall subject matter read in mathematics. Students then should be asked to say aloud meanings attached to mathematical content read. In this way, the learner becomes increasingly aware of the necessity in paying careful attention to what was read in mathematical subject matter. Understanding of ideas is the only reason for reading content (Dymock, 2007).

From literal comprehension of subject-matter, students sequentially need to be develop skills to read analytically. This pertains to evaluating what has been read in terms of quality standards. Reading analytically involves separating subject matter read into component parts to notice if it harmonizes with reputable statements of accuracy. When solving a problem in mathematics, students need to separate the relevant from the irrelevant. Higher levels of cognition are then involved. Then too, subject-matter read permits the student to think of ensuing ideas in a unique way. Originality is vital in creative thought such as thinking of a new solution to a mathematics problem (Ediger, 2002).

IN CONCLUSION

A professional mathematics teacher has a plethora of tools to use in emphasizing effective instruction. It takes time, effort, and desire in becoming a truly effective instructor. The teacher needs to take part in relevant experiences in workshops,

Constructivism in the Mathematics Curriculum

Somewhat opposite of data driven instruction is constructivism. Constructivists (Vygotsky, 1978) greatly minimize the use of tests to ascertain pupil achievement and progress. Teacher observation on a continual basis is used to assist learners in mathematics. Jean Piaget emphasized an individualized approach in using constructivism as a psychology of learning whereas Len Vygotsky stressed the use of small group endeavors. Thus the math teacher observes when and where pupils need help. The assistance generally is not given in terms of an explanation or lecture, but rather questions are raised by the teacher leading the pupil to arrive at correct answers. The math teacher has a thorough grasp of subject matter in assisting pupils to come up with what is accurate. The processes and answers are equally salient in mathematics. If word problems are being stressed, the teacher assists pupils in determining unrecognized words by :

- helping the pupil use context clues in correctly identifying a word
- using phonics in identifying the initial consonant of a word and then notching sequential letters with corresponding sounds
- divide an unknown word into syllables, prefixes/ suffixes, and noticing a shorter word within the longer word (Ediger, 2009)

The above-listed asterisked items are utilized to recognize an unknown word and then to attach meaning to subject-matter read. They are not used, for example, to emphasize learning phonics for its own sake, but used to attach meaning to mathematical subject-matter being read.

Constructivism emphasizes that pupils appraise their own individual progress with teacher assistance. Learning is sequential in the minds of pupils, not in the mind of the teacher. The pupil orders new experiences which are directly related to previously learned content. The following kinds of learning opportunities provide pupils with activities to sequence their very own subject-matter and skills with mathematics teacher guidance :

- problem solving which stresses deliberation and intrinsic effort
- project methods stressing construction of objects and items
- making of geometrical models (Dewey, 1916).

In each of the above asterisked items, the learning experience moves for ward without specific objectives for each facet and stage of achievement. Mistakes are made along the way and are rectified by learners in context, not as separate items to be tested. The teacher of mathematics is there to guide, motivate, and encourage, in authentic learnings, but not to tell pupils how to proceed. He/she may model an authentic task prior to learners being actively engaged. Modeling is done to clarify task engagement to pupils. Learning by discovery is a key point to emphasize in constructivist thinking.

References

Dewey, John (1916), *Democracy and Education.* New York: Macmillan Company.

Ediger, Marlow (1989), "Psychology of Teaching Mathematics," (1989), *Delta* K, 27 (4), 20-23.

Ediger, Marlow (2006), "Writing in the Mathematics Curriculum," *Journal of Instructional Psychology*," 33 (1), 120-123.

Ediger, Marlow (2007), "Readiness for Mathematics Learning and the Student," *Experiments in Education*, 35(8), 1-5.

Ediger, Marlow (2009), For An Effective Reading Program," *Reading Improvement*, 46 (3), 119-122.

- accompanying Manual and its uses.

Teacher written tests are salient to use at selected intervals to measure achievement. Multiple choice test items should possess the following standards :

- each test item should generally have four distractors.
- the distractors should be of simulator length so that clues are minimized/eliminated as to the correct response.
- the stem and each of the four distractors should make for a grammatically correct sentence.
- no pattern should exist in terms of which is the correct response.

Face validity may be used when writing teacher written tests. Thus, after a concept or generalization has been taught, the mathematics teacher may then apply the same content in writing a test item. Clarity and meaning must be inherent in each test item written. Few teachers use test/retest approaches to check reliability. *Reliability* emphasizes that a test measure consistently. Test/retest reliability means giving the same test two times within a few days apart to notice if learners, basically, received thesame/similar percentile or number of correct test responses. If the scores differ much from one testing to the next for the same pupil, the chances are the test times are vague or do not measure what was taught, among other factors. *Alternative forms* reliability emphasizes the mathematics teacher write two separate tests covering-objectives in the lesson or unit of study taught. Teachers generally do not have the needed time to do this. However, split half reliability requires administering the teacher written test once, and then comparing the even numbered with the odd numbered responses for all pupils in a class. Does the test measure consistently in that generally Pupil A is highest in both the odd/even comparison; pupil B is second high whereas pupil C is third high, and so on.

Teacher written essay test items may do a good job of assessing mathematics achievement if selected criteria are met such as the following :

- the items are written on the understanding level of pupils. If reading is a problem, the teacher may read the test items aloud. The writer when teaching in a two teacher rural school had two seventh graders in one grade level only. It did not take long to notice that reading caused difficulties in solving word problems; these were then read aloud to the two pupils who then did fairly well on the arithmetic facet.
- essay test items need to be delimited, but not to the point of requiring factual answers. Thus, a problem solving approach is recommenced whereby pupils need to deliberate and think to ascertain answers. Problems in mathematics need to involve indepth thought in which critical and creative thinking are involved.
- the test length should measure objectives stressed in class, but not to the length whereby learner fatigue sets in when responding. The purpose is to measure mathematical problem solving skills and not endurance.
- pupils may show procedures used in problem solving. Mathematics teachers might then view how pupils responded as well as the answer obtained. This provides feedback to the teacher as to what needs reteaching and emphasis necessary to optimize pupil achievement.

There are additional avenues of collaborative thinking in improving teacher evaluation in the mathematics curriculum. These include teacher observation of learner performance. Collaboration here must stress how observation of pupils in ongoing math lessons and units of study can be made more effective. The following should be considered carefully :

- Are the objectives relevant for learners in school and in society, as well as for those going into the professions?
- Do they stress a balance between subject matter knowledge and skills in mathematics?
- Are they arranged sequentially in moving from what is taught and understood to those which are gradually more complex?
- Is meaning making and deriving sense in ensuing mathematical lessons being emphasized?
- Are attitudinal objectives being stressed adequately?

Collaboration in studying and evaluating objectives in mathematics is time well spent. The objectives need to possess clarity and stated in measurable terms so that it may be ascertained if, after instruction, they have been attained by pupils. Periodical review of what is taught leads to a better understanding of what pupils are experiencing and which innovations need to be advocated. With collaboration, mathematics teachers might well try out revised objectives in their classrooms and report back to the group how well teaching and learning transpired. Problems identified here need study and recommendations made to further improve the mathematics curriculum.

Learning opportunities for pupils to achieve the objectives also need indepth study by participants in collaborative endeavors. Learning opportunities must be varied to provide for each pupil so that he/she may attain as optimally as possible. Different kinds of learning opportunities need to be discussed to determine what works and what changes/ modifications need to be made. Active participation in collaborative endeavors may be fostered by paying attention to *relevant,* not trivial, items in teaching and learning situations. Video tapes of classroom teaching might well provide a basis for analyzing teacher and pupil behaviors in mathematical units of study. The following identified problem areas need consideration :

- What should be the role of the latest in technology in the math curriculum?
- Must inservice education be emphasized to assist mathematics teachers to fully utilize technology to assist pupils in meaningful leanings?
- Which additional kinds of technology, than those possessed, are necessary to aid in the instructional arena?
- Would an increased use of technology stimulate pupil interest in ongoing experiences in the classroom?
- What is the role of more traditional procedures in teaching such as carefully chosen textbooks, workbooks, and work sheets?

The mathematics teacher models quality attitudes toward content, skills, and an appreciation for efforts made by mathematicians in developing knowledge and skills in the mathematical arena. It is vital for teachers to keep up with the latest developments in the teaching of mathematics. Technology continues to come out at a rapid rate and teachers must be aware of what will assist pupils to do well in math achievement. Learning by discovery, problem solving, as well as creative and critical thinking need to permeate the math curriculum.

Collaboration by teachers in assessing pupil achievement is vital. Certainly, a quality assessment program is necessary. With standardized testing, math teachers need to attach meaning to the following concepts pertaining to assessment:

- validity of the test and how its is determined
- reliability and its role in the development of tests
- the definition of standardized tests
- formative and summative evaluation as well as measuring benchmarks of pupil progress

National Council Teachers of Mathematics (1989), *Curriculum and Evaluation Standards for School Mathematics*. Reston, Va.: NCTM.

Newton, Xiaoxia (2007), "Reflections of Mathematics Reform," *Phi Delta Kappan*, 27 (4), 20-23.

Vygotsky, Len (1978), Mind In Society: *The Development of Higher Psychological Processes*. Cambridge, Massachusets: Harvard University Press.

11 CHAPTER

Collaboration in Improving Mathematics Curriculum

By working together mathematics teachers and supervisors can do much to improve teaching and learning in mathematics. Collaboration is important to develop high quality objectives, learning opportunities, and appraisal procedures in teaching pupils. Each participant needs to be well informed of recommended procedures, research, and technology in instructional settings.

A special section in the school library needs to house instructional materials for mathematics teachers. Thus, university level teaching of mathematics textbooks, professional mathematics teaching journals, different series of math textbooks K-12, video tapes on mathematics instruction, among other references sources need to be available for teacher referral and use.

Curriculum Improvement in Mathematics

With the team approach, participants may share ideas and engage in higher levels of cognition to solve problems in teaching mathematics. There are a plethora of points of intervention. First, the objectives of instruction need scrutiny in terms of raising the following questions :

- examples of knowledge to be used in highly specific procedures to solve mathematical problems. Indepth math knowledge needs to be used here. Too frequently, this may be lacking when arriving at a solution.
- ways of assisting pupils to learn inductively.
- emphasizing mathematical reasoning in observations made.
- recording dated observations and summarizing results.
- filing observational data for each pupil to be used in making subsequent comparisons.

There are a plethora of means to use collaborative thinking in the mathematics curriculum. Working together harmoniously, mathematics teachers may collaboratively solve problems pertaining to objectives, learning opportunities, and appraisal procedures.

12

CHAPTER

Factors that Assist Mathematics Achievement

There are selected factors which might well help pupil achievement in mathematics. These need to be studied, and analyzed and conclusions realized. Public schools need to possess a special place where quality video tapes, teaching mathematics journals and university level mathematics education textbooks, internet, and web sources are available to acquire relevant knowledge and skills to use in ongoing units of study in the classroom. The psychology of learning, among other factors, must be stressed in teaching and learning situations in order to optimize achievement and progress in mathematics. Thus, pupils need to connect subject to the self, to experiences in society, and to the school setting.

Class Size and Learner Progress

How might a class be organized so that pupils may benefit from instruction? This appears to be a perennial question. Hopefully, class size will not. exceed approximately, 20-25 pupils. This should make it possible to teach all pupils effectively.

Pupils may be taught in large group instruction. To initiate a new mathematical unit of study, the teacher must use teaching materials which are clearly visible to all in the classroom. Needed materials of teaching may include a large place value chart with paper strips to show ones, tens, hundreds, and thousands values, as well as congruent objects to be used as markers indicating place value. The mathematics teacher may then demonstrate to pupils how to regroup and rename in addition and subtraction. He/she observes pupils carefully to notice that each is listening carefully and noticing how this is done. The learnings are paced and sequential so that learners individually have opportunities to acquire facts, concepts, and generalizations necessary to perform these operations successfully. The mathematics teacher observes pupils carefully to notice engagement as each attends, watches, and notices poignant learnings.

Next, the teacher divides pupils into groups of four. These may be heterogeneous or homogeneous depending upon the purpose involved. Each set of four receives a sheet of problems and a smaller place value chart to practice the objectives emphasized in the larger group. The teacher circulates among the committees to notice time on task behaviours as well as meanings pupils attach to place value. Interests of pupils is noticed within each small group and the quality of interactions is also observed. The teacher then carefully monitors achievement to notice what pupils do not understand with assistance given as needed to overcome problem areas. However, it is good to have pupils ponder and discuss indepth necessary ideas in regrouping and renaming. Selected pupils learn best in social situations whereby ideas circulate within a small group of learners.The mathematics teacher records and dates problem areas as well as progress made by pupils using anecdotal approaches.

Cooperative teaching may also be used whereby involved teachers work together to plan sequential lessons. Here, teachers take turns in teaching the large group made up of two or three classrooms of children. This makes inservice education more readily available in that teachers may observe each other teach and offer comments for improvement. Smaller groupings of four or five pupils might then work on problems subsequent to large group instruction. Cooperating teachers might then circulate among committees to offer assistance as needed to foster learner interest and meaning in the ongoing activity.

Individual needs must be met, based on the large and small group endeavours. It is good to document needs of pupils which were noticed in the previous grouping arrangements. Each anecdotal statement then is dated per pupil and necessary help given as listed. The mathematics teacher needs to have needed indepth subject matter and pedagogy in mind in order to offer quality guidance. Mastery learning is salient. Pupils individually must attain sequentially. What is not understood needs remedying so that a solid foundation is built for acquiring ensuing mathematical facts, concepts, and generalizations. Too frequently, the teacher has hurried and moved rapidly to cover content in the basal textbook with little attention paid to learner achievement of each step of progress in an ongoing unit of study.

Inservice Growth

Mathematics teachers must possess the needed knowledge to implement high quality strategies of instruction. Growth and achievement is ongoing in teaching. Thus, the public school should have a convenient place for mathematics teachers to study and converse with colleagues on mathematics content and effective means of instruction. In this area for study, there should be recent mathematics journals, yearbooks, and paperbacks published by the National Council Teachers of Mathematics, among others. Encouragement must be given by school administrators for teachers to read and implement ideas which meet standards of quality. The same would be true for housing university level mathematical teacher education texts.

Math teachers may meet together to analyze content and pedagogical methods to improve the curriculum. The dates for meetings and the math literature or topics to be discussed need to be agreed upon. Teachers, also, must elaborate on what has worked well for them pertaining to that used in teaching and learning situations in ongoing lessons and units of study. The doors of effective communication need to be opened among teachers so that good ideas circulate among group members. Trust and consideration for each other is vital. Mathematics teachers and pupils are poignant in the total educational enterprise. Thus, the processes of group work need emphasis. Each can learn much from others and motivate cooperative endeavours. Enthusiasm for learning might well be a motivator to build morale among committee members. New ideas be that motivator to increase energy levels for teaching mathematics!

Mathematics teachers need to engage in self-reflection in which they :

- rehearse what was achieved previously in teaching pupils in noticing that which may be done differently to optimize progress.
- take careful notice of what is needed personally in inservice education to improve teaching performance.
- become increasingly proficient in managing grouping procedures as well as learner behaviour.
- must think in terms of continuous improvement of the self as well as of pupils in mathematical content and skills.

Teachers of mathematics need to develop favourable attitudes in curriculum endeavours. A good self-concept must be attained. Thus, self-efficacy is a salient goal in that :

- teachers feel competent in teaching pupils of a variety of achievement and ability levels
- the latest technology can be used very effectively to enhance pupil learning.
- they can provide, fully, for individual differences among learners including children of poverty and from diverse cultures.
- teaching methods can be used which are beneficial to all English Language Learners (ELL) regardless of language proficiency.
- definite provisions can be made to teach diverse categories of handicapped pupils.
- mathematics teachers exhibit pride in their profession when communicating with others.

Mathematics may be integrated with other academic areas, for example, such as the social studies in that learners study Egyptian and Roman systems of numeration; and in science whereby mathematics is the language of the physical sciences as in force, distance, and work performed given in numerical terms. Integration is stressed when there is a need to do so and it assists pupils to understand relevant facts, concepts, and generalizations.

Evaluation of Achievement

There are selected methods of achievement which need to be used to assess learner progress. Mandated testing occurs once a year and involves the use of standardized tests. Thus, pupils for any grade level have the same directions, time limits, and the same scoring key used in computerized scoring. Validity and reliability data are given in the Manual for each test taken by pupils in the pilot study. The mathematics teacher's pupils score from test results is then compared with those in the Manual to ascertain percentile ranking and/or grade equivalent. Numerical data are then obtained to learn about each pupil's achievement as well as average achievement for a classroom and/or school system. From all testing situations, the teacher needs to use printouts/feedback to notice what needs more emphasis. Errors made by pupils stress the need for remedial work in terms of processes and products. Standardized tests are generally given once a school year; thus, in the mean time, teacher made tests also play a vital role in instruction.

Teacher written tests may also include multiple choice test items whereby the stem with one distractor of four given is correct. However, teacher written tests should include essay items; these include problem solving which broadens pupil's knowledge and skills by having authentic word problems to solve. Here, pupils need to show their work in arriving at the correct answer. The advantages of having pupils show processes include the following :

- the teacher may notice thought processes involved by pupils and thus aid is provided to assist pupils in remediation
- he/she may notice algorithms used by pupils in problem-solving
- reading difficulties in solving word problems
- incorrect copying of numerals making for errors
- illegible handwriting making for difficulties to track pupil progress in doing problem solving.

Teacher observation using quality standards of evaluation of pupil work in ongoing lessons, on a daily basis stresses :

- the importance of assisting pupils when difficulties arise in computation and problem solving. With assistance, adequate time must be given for pupils to analyze, synthesize, and evaluate, to become self sufficient in remedying difficulties.
- noticing difficulties in individual learner processes to stress remediation in large and small group sessions.

IN CONCLUSION

The mathematics curriculum continues to change in terms of subject matter emphasis and methodology in teaching. Quality inservice education is needed to stress the best of objectives for pupil attainment, means for learners to attain these objectives, and appraisal techniques. Education is ongoing and subject to continuous change. Thus, there will always be a need for continuous education.

13 CHAPTER

Portfolios in Mathematics Curriculum

Portfolios might well be an excellent approach for pupils and mathematics teachers to share the former's achievement with parents, as well as with other interested, responsible persons. Here, parents may observe and evaluate pupil progress authentically. Parents then may view learner achievement directly from pupil products, not from test scores. Questions arise and answers given in assessing the products. The valid concerns of parents might become a part of the portfolio.

A plethora of mathematics products may become a part of the portfolio. They represent efforts, motivation, and pupil purposes in ongoing lessons and units of study. Here, the pupil is actively engaged in choosing what to include in a portfolio. He/she is not a passive recipient, but evaluates, learns, grows and develops in the process. Too frequently, pupils merely respond to test items given on the local, state, and national levels. From test results, the pupil passively views a percentile, grade equivalent, or per cent given for correct answers given. In doing a portfolio, the pupil selects representative inclusions. It is flexible and open ended in terms of its development (Kasinath, 2009).

Philosophy of Portfolio Development

Constructivism, as a psychology of learning, emphasizes that the pupil is in charge of his/her learning activities. As an active learner, the pupils sequences his/her own experiences. The mathematics teacher is a facilitator and guide, not a lecturer. He/she observes and assists pupils to learn by discovery. The mathematics teacher sets the stage in introducing new subject matter.New learnings are developed by pupils in moving from the known to the unknown. If a learner needs help on a new process in mathematics, the teacher raises questions which lead pupils to the correct response. Telling is not teaching, but scaffolding based on background information guides each pupil to achieve more optimally. Thus, the pupil develops his/her own knowledge within a learning sequence (Ediger, 2010).

Constructivism emphasizes the uniqueness of the learner with his/her own background knowledge and culture. Responsibility for achieving in mathematics resides within the pupil. The teacher encourages each pupil to achieve in mathematics, but motivation is intrinsic and comes from within the learner. Teaching is facilitating learning and there is a dynamic interaction among the learning activity, the mathematics teacher, and the pupil. For example, within an ongoing unit of study pertaining to place value, properties of four basic operations, fractions, decimals, regrouping and renaming, estimation, statistics and probability, as well as fundamental learnings in algebra and geometry, the pupil together with the facilitator, and curriculum interact; they are not separate entities (Wotk, 2008).

Testing is very frequently used to ascertain pupil achievement in mathematics. Here, the learner is a somewhat passive individual, responding to multiple choice test items. Portfolio develop emphasizes the learner being actively involved in choosing entries from daily work completed within lessons and units of study. A random sampling is chosen by the pupil with teacher facilitation. A Table of Contents brings order to these dated entries and makes it easier for parents, teachers, and other responsible individuals to peruse and evaluate mathematical learnings developed by a pupil. The following are examples of what may become a part of a mathematics portfolio :

- daily work completed in ongoing lessons and units of study.
- line, bar, and circle graphs as well as charts made such as a narrative which tells the history of number and its uses, a tabulation chart which indicates growth and comparisons in population figures of selected countries integrated with the social studies, an organizational chart indicating structure and order in base ten numeration, and pictured graphs in chart form, among others.
- objects constructed such as a place value chart, a fact finder, beanstalks to show sets of different values, and a fraction/decimal chart.
- games developed such as addition, subtraction, and multiplication bingo.
- electronic photos of constructed items such as geoboards and tangrams.
- drawings of geometrical models, attribute blocks, as well as other manipulative materials.
- recordings of pupils involved in small group discussions (Ediger, 2005).

The above are examples of what might constitute a portfolio of pupil work and products. Active pupil, involvement necessitates the choosing of contents for the portfolio. He/she owns the portfolio and shares its selection of entries with the facilitator/teacher. The portfolio, too, provides a basis for doing parent/teacher conferences. Here, the learner may play a leadership role in discussing achievement within the conference. What has been accomplished and what is left to learn is diagnostic as well as remedial and promotes developmental learnings.

Somewhat opposite of constructivism and portfolio development is behaviorism. Behaviorism stresses the following :

- establishing measurable objectives for pupils to attain in mathematics.
- aligning learning opportunities with the stated objectives.
- teaching toward pupils attaining these objectives (Ediger, 2003).

A deductive approach is generally used in teaching mathematics. Content moves from the teacher to pupils with the end result being for the latter to achieve behaviorally stated objectives. Testing is a major procedure used to ascertain pupil progress. Pupil results are indicated through precise numerical results such as percentiles and grade equivalents (See Gardner, 1993).

Constructivism, Dewey, Piaget, and Vygotsky

Three highly recognized constructivists are John Dewey, Jean Piaget, and Len Vygotsky. Dewey (1916) emphasized a problem solving curriculum whereby the pupil with teacher guidance would identify a problem within a unit of study. Pupils need to have necessary background information to delve into securing a possible solution. The problem needs adequate delimitation so that it can be solved. There are a plethora of practical problems in mathematics which need to be identified. These require deliberation and thought, not a factual answer. For example, a classroom is securing new carpeting. The problem then pertains to securing the number of square feet or square yards for the covering. Pupils initially might hypothesize how to ascertain the approximate answer. They are actively involved here as they are in sequential steps of solving a problem. The teacher may raise questions as needed to assist pupils in mathematical problem-solving. After deliberation, pupils may check their hypothesis of necessary skills to ascertain the answer as well as evaluate the correctness of the answer. There is interaction, here, between the pupil, the teacher, and the curriculum. This might be an individual or small group endeavour.

Jean Piaget (1973) stressed a maturation theory of learning whereby the pupil develops different capabilities of thought as he/she progresses in age and through the grades in school.

There were four stages of pupil development as Piaget's research indicated :

- sensori-motor, ages birth to eighteen months of age
- preoperational, eighteen months to seven years
- concrete operations, seven to eleven years of age
- formal operations, twelve years and older.

In each of the above-named years, pupils change and modify their perceptions. Thus, from birth to eighteen months of age, pupils need to experience concrete objects and items. Learning occurs through viewing, interacting, and observing. In the preoperational stage, the pupil also experiences the concrete, but perceives each by seeing one variable at a time. The stage of concrete operations emphasizes blending the concrete with increasingly more abstract learnings such as physical representations with numbers/numerals. Whereas, the stage of formal operations stresses that pupils can reason through abstract methods in using numbers/numerals in addition, multiplication, subtraction, and division. Reasoning and inventing have become leading approaches in learning as well as critical, creative thinking, and problem solving. Piaget emphasized that *individually* the pupil arrived at each stage maturationally and was assisted through each stage with adult/teacher guidance.

Vygotsky emphasized that learning was a social situation, not individually based. Thus, within a committee or small group pupils worked together on a project. Members learn from each other when interacting and ideas "bounce off the minds" of participants. The teacher facilitates learning among group members, but does not, by any means, dominate the participation. The small group progresses with active participation and ideas are modified within the committee. By challenging and modifying ideas presented, committee members benefit in developing comprehensive structures (Vygotsky, 1978).

Commonalities in psychological/philosophical thinking involving John Dewey, Jean Piaget, and Len Vygotsky are the following :

- the teacher is a facilitator of learning and not a "sage on the stage".
- pupils own the curriculum with the teacher assisting learner achievement and progress.
- pupils construct knowledge and acquisition does not come from lecture or the teacher indoctrinating with what is correct.
- sequence in achieving resides within the pupil, not the materials of instruction.
- pupils interact among themselves, the materials of instruction, and the teacher. There is interaction not dominatfon. With the thinking of Jean Piaget, however, the pupil develops largely through maturation.

References

Dewey, John (1916), *Democracy in Education.* New York: The Macmillan Company.

Ediger, Marlow (2003), *Teaching Mathematics Successfully.* New Delhi, India : Discovery Publishing House.

Ediger, Marlow (2010), "Portfolios in Science," *Virginia Journal of Science Education*, 3 (2), 12.

Ediger, Marlow (2005), "Teaching Mathematics in the School Setting," *College Student Journal*, 39 (4), 711-715.

Gardner, Howard (1993), *Multiple Intelligences: Theory Into Practice.* New York : Basic Books.

Kasinath, H. M. (2009), "Nature of Knowledge in Constructivism, Implications for Education," *Journal of Community Guidance and Research*, 26 (3), 259-266.

Piaget, Jean (1973), To Understand Is To Invent. New York: Grossman.

Vygotsky, Len S. (1978), *Mind In Society*. Cambridge, Massachusetts: Harvard University Press.

Wolk, S. (2008), "Joy in School," *Educational Leadership*, 66 (1), 8-14.

14

CHAPTER

Enjoyment in Mathematics Curriculum

Wholesome attitudes are salient to develop in any curriculum area, mathematics being no exception. Many pupils like mathematics; others may not develop this quality attitude. The attitudinal dimension is salient to develop in school and in society. Higher accomplishments are then possible. With good attitudes, achievement in mathematics can be optimized.

Too frequently, mathematics may become routine and drudgery. This certainly need not be so. A motivated teacher may select and implement those activities which provide enjoyment at the same time objectives of instruction are being acquired. Enjoyment and achievement of objectives need not be separated from each other, but can well become integrated entities (Ediger, 2006).

The Affective Dimension in Teaching and Learning

The pupil is the focal point of instruction. He/she needs to perceive mathematics as being positive, useful, and good. The learner experiences and reaches conclusions. Hopefully, the learner will develop positive feelings of wanting to learn more mathematical content and skills. These inward feelings should result. The teacher designs and implements what was planned for teaching and learning experiences. The interest factor must be thoroughly considered with the following in mind :

- providing a variety of activities such as those requiring a hands on approach with real objects in doing the four basic operations of addition, subtraction, multiplication, and division.
- emphasis also being placed upon visual representations of reality including pictorial forms, computerized programs with illustrations, video tape, and power point slides, showing, for example, geometrical figures, plane and solid geometry, as well as calculations involving reasoning and problem solving. The writer when supervising university student teachers in the public schools observed an interesting lesson on geometry art for young children. The supervising teacher and the student teacher cut geometrical figures from different colours of construction paper. Pupils selected geometrical figures to portray people, buildings, among other items, on drawing paper. The products were posted on the bulletin board for viewing. Pupils had to name each figure as being a circle, square, triangle, rhombus, etc. Pupils from other classrooms came in to observe and comment on the geometry art project. Enthusiasm and interest were high.
- abstractions which indicate how the real and the pictorial may be represented numerically and used in school/society. For example, a picture graph was developed by pupils showing a photo of each in the month of birth. Other picture graphs were shown and discussed; pupils developed an understanding of why graphs are used to present data (Kennedy and Tipps, 1991).

Interest factors involve wholehearted involvement by learners. Well-planned lessons with appropriate use of teaching aids assist pupils in enjoying mathematics. The mathematics teacher's modulated voice with proper stress of words, pitch within sentences, and juncture (pauses) attract learner attention to achieve objectives of instruction. Gestures should be positive and harmonize with deeds. The following personality traits need to be in the offing :

- politeness and respect
- caring and helpfulness
- positive attitudes toward teaching and learning
- feelings of excitement toward mathematics
- wanting to learn more about mathematical content
- willingness to work harmoniously with parents (Brady, 2008).

If the teacher sequences learning opportunities, he/she must take care to have it be developmental appropriate. If a pupil does not understand a mathematical process due to its difficulty, it might well hinder positive affective development whereas if it is too easy, then boredom might well set in. The mathematics teacher then has a problem in selecting learning opportunities which are developmentally appropriate. A pupil may attain a somewhat difficult learning through scaffolding whereby the teacher builds upon pupil knowledge possessed and then assists the learner to achieve the more complex mathematical understanding using cues, techniques, and experiences which help the pupil to achieve what formerly was too complex. Each step of learning, however, must be challenging and learner centered. The interests of pupils might well be cultivated through a challenging mathematical curriculum (Cuban, 2008).

Adequate time, too, must be given to help pupils reflect upon what was learned. Metacognition emphasizes concepts pertaining to "thinking about thinking". Thus, the pupil needs assistance to reflect upon past mathematical experiences. The teacher might demonstrate aloud how metacognition operates to retain and strengthen understandings acquired. What is not understood is brought to the forefront and provides opportunities for meaningful clarification and reteaching. With meaning attached to ongoing teaching and learning experiences, pupils understand subject-matter taught.

Pupils are then ready to build new facts, concepts, and generalizations based on previously understood content. Mastery of mathematical algorithms provides readiness to achieve new objectives of instruction. Indepth learning aids the pupil to understand, grow, accomplish, and achieve. Interest, too, is furthered with the pupil truly attaching meaning to subsequent learnings (Ediger, 2008).

Self-efficacy is enhanced when teachers become increasingly knowledgeable of subject-matter and skills. Confidence is then developed in the self. The mathematics teacher secures feelings of being able to teach and provide for pupils of different categories such as the gifted, English Language Learners, slow learners, and the mentally retarded. There is this feeling of being successful in teaching a variety of kinds of pupils. Each pupil needs to attain as optimally as possible.

To possess feelings of enjoyment, pupils, too, need to feel that purpose is involved in learning. Reasons are then accepted for achieving salient objectives of instruction. How might the mathematics teacher assist pupils to perceive purpose in learning?

- to indicate relevancy in an ongoing lesson. For example, when pupils are studying how to determine area, they need help to see practical uses which can be made of the concept. Memorization, alone, does not guide pupils to perceive purpose. They need to understand each sequential step of learning, as well as perceive uses which can be made in school and in society. Uses to be made in finding the area include measuring classroom size, length and width, to notice the size of carpet which needs to be installed. The number of square feet, for example, may be meaningfully made by marking off squares, one foot by one foot, in the classroom. Pupils may then count the number of squares. The number of counted squares may be compared with taking the length of squares times the width of the squares which then equals the area of the classroom. Concrete and life like experiences assist pupils to use numerical values to represent reality. Sequential learning and practicality are two concepts which provide readiness for future accomplishments. The teacher must observe to notice that each sequence is meaningful and understood, resulting in the ultimate purpose of the learning, to determine the area of square feet in the classroom.

- to encourage the use of games to interest learners in mathematics. Computerize games are intriguing to many pupils if they are developmentally appropriate. The writer when supervising university student teachers has observed many pupils playing math games via the computer. Intrinsically, these are motivating to learners. Pupils respond to a problem on the monitor and then receive immediate feedback as to it correctness. Independently, the pupil may move forward sequentially on one or more games. Wholesome competition might also be brought in between opposing sides in attempting to be a winner. Computer programs may be used, also, as simulation, tutorial, drill and practice, and diagnostic/ remediation. They need to be integrated into the regular mathematics curriculum (Ediger, 2009).

Pupils, too, have been fascinated with teacher made mathematics games. Here, the games are, ideally, aligned with the objectives in an ongoing unit of study. Order and sequence are built into each game, with enjoyment being a leading goal. Games assist pupils to review and rehearse previously acquired learnings. Active involvement of learners in gaming as well as in all learning activities is salient!

WHAT TO AVOID

Enjoyment, among others, must be a major goal for pupils to achieve in mathematics learning. Thus, there need to be pitfalls to avoid in the curriculum. The pitfalls include the following :

- **criticism of pupils.** Rather, what pupils do not understand should be clarified and appropriate learning activities used to remedy deficiencies.
- **impatience.** Too frequently, too much ground is being covered from basal textbooks in order to complete activities in a hurry, resulting in shallow learnings. Instead, a quality indepth sequence needs to be in the offing so that new subject matter taught is based on previously well understood facts, concepts, and generalizations.
- **rudeness and rude comments.** If pupils do not attain as well as desired, the teacher must not ridicule learners but needs to examine his/her own procedures of instruction. A variety of learning opportunities must be used to assist pupils to achieve, grow, and develop. Remedying deficiencies is needed to correct inaccurate learnings of pupils. This must be followed by using a developmental strategy of instruction.

References

Brady, Marion (2008), "Cover the Material—Or Teach Children to Think," 65, (5), 64-67.

Cuban, Larry (2008), "The Perennial Reform: Fixing School Time," *Phi Delta Kappan*, 90 (4), 240-250.

Ediger, Marlow (2006), "Writing in the Mathematics Curriculum," *Journal of Instructional Psychology*, 33 (1), 120-123.

Ediger, Marlow (2008), "Modern School Mathematics," *The College Student Journal*, 42 (4), 986-989.

Ediger, Marlow (2009),, "The Principal in the Teaching and Learning Process," *Education*, 129 (4), 574-578.

Kennedy, Leonard M., and Steve Tipps (1991), *Guiding Children's Learning of Mathematics*. Belmont, California: Wadsworth Publishing Company.

15

CHAPTER

Computer-aided Instruction in Mathematics Curriculum

A very common approach of teaching mathematics emphasizes the use of a carefully chosen textbook as a guide to follow in student instruction. Diverse audio-visual aids may be used to enrich and clarify experiences. The methods of teaching used may incorporate deductive, inductive, and problem-solving procedures. Students are tested along the way with formative tests to indicate how well they have mastered the material at a given point in time. Ultimately, a summative test might well be given to notice learner progress and achievement for the entire unit of instruction. A mandated test may also be required to reveal how well the student is achieving the objectives of the local state. This in a nut shell describes the general way of mathematics instruction followed by classroom teachers. In contrast, the balance of this paper will discuss computer-aided instruction (CAI) as well as elaborate on basal textbook procedures.

The Student and Computerized Instruction

In CAI, mathematics instruction is strongly geared to the individual student. Meeting the math needs of individual students must receive priority. Students need to pace learnings at their own unique optimal rate of achievement. The mathematical content must be relevant and useful in school and in society. A well-developed program needs to be on the developmental level of the learner so that he/she may achieve as optimally as possible (Ediger and Rao, 2001).

The teacher needs to be passionate and enthusiastic about mathematics and the math curriculum. A conscientious indepth study of computerized programmes/packages needs to be made to ascertain which are best suitable for a given set of learners, as well as for individual students. Careful consideration in selecting computer packages should follow the ensuing criteria:

- the level of mathematical content difficulty is appropriate for subject-matter acquisition
- math vocabulary terms assist students to attach meaning to ongoing experiences
- accuracy of subject matter is inherent in each package and does not contain stereotypes offensive to any human being
- purpose for each software package possesses clarity
- quality sequence is emphasized in that students are successful achievers in its use
- graphics, colour, and sound, promote the learning of mathematics
- each program motivates students to achieve, grow, and learn
- feedback to learners' responses provides necessary and valuable information for the ensuing item to be learned (Djeassilane, 2008).

The above named criteria provide guidance and direction in selecting software programmes in mathematics for students to attain vital objectives of instruction. The subject matter content needs to be meaningful and understandable. The level of vocabulary difficulty must enable the learner to achieve in valuable mathematical knowledge. Each computer program needs to have content which meets the standard of being entirely accurate. The order of subject-matter knowledge must be such that each student is successful in making progress. Challenging, but achieveable content, needs to be in the offing. Peripherals must assist students to achieve and not hinder learner concentration on the task at hand. From test results, the student must receive usable feedback which promotes future learning. The CAI programmes may assist in evaluating student readiness for new learnings through pre-testing. Computerized subject-matter content is then more likely to be presented in an achievable form. Drill items assist learners to retain knowledge. Drill needs to promote interest in learning and not minimize it. These programs may be game based drill items to assist learners to enjoy and appreciate mathematics. Post-test items are given to ascertain specifically what has been learned by students. Test information is then stored for future use by the mathematics teacher (Ediger, 2005).

The CAI makes it possible to have self-directed learning. The student then interacts with software in a computer. Responses that students make from content on the monitor provide data to the machine as to which subject matter comes next in sequence. The next sequential mathematical item should then be on the achievement level of the student. The opportunities to be a successful learner are indeed great. Without computerized math instruction, the teacher may move forward too rapidly or too slowly in aiding learner achievement, either through lecture or a discussion. In computerized math learnings, the next sequential item presented on the monitor is based on the level of success experienced in the previous item. Readiness for the ensuing learning is then based on previously acquired knowledge (Ediger, 2006).

There is efficiency in teaching when students experience much success in achieving knowledge goals in mathematics.

Failure and mistakes are minimized. CAI never grows tired, nor disgusted with students in developing knowledge and skills. It promotes interaction between the computer and the student on an individualized basis, much like a tutor and a child. It is designed to meet the mathematical needs of a student. It is learner centered in providing for individual differences. The pace of learning is determined by the student (National Council Teachers of Mathematics, 1989),

Feedback from test results assists pupils to notice progress and achievement. The learner then notices what needs further help in mathematics knowledge and skill. Diagnosis and prescription will assist the learner to remedy that which needs remediating so that further progress is in evidence. CAI, basically, is an automated method of teaching whereby the learner and the computer interact to achieve objectives of instruction. The following steps are followed in designing CAI programmes :

- evaluating the present status of a student's achievement with a pre-test.
- providing mathematical subject matter in a meaningful manner.
- presenting drill and practice activities to fix knowledge in the mind of the learner.
- assisting pupil interest in learning with a gaming approach.
- assessing student achievement by using a post test.
- walking learners through a sequence of software teaching packages.
- keeping a record of test scores to notice student achievement (Wiske, 2004).

The CAI may emphasize simulations whereby a reality basis situation is placed into a computer program. Simulation might then be integrated with other less reality based programmes that are abstract in nature. Simulation may show the stages of an insect in complete metamorphoses. Thus, for example in sequence, the egg, larva, pupa, and adult may be shown in life like manner on the monitor, as these changes occur.

The CAI is one mode of instruction which can meet the personal needs of students in mathematics. The styles of learning differ among learners in the classroom. Brief mention was made in this manuscript initially of the basal textbook method. The writer, in supervising university student teachers in the public schools, noticed many pupils who did well in mathematics using this method of learning. A well prepared and enthusiastic teacher can also do much to assist pupil achievement. Here, the class as a whole, committees, and individual study may be used to assist pupils to achieve objectives in mathematics. Audiovisual aids may be used in large group instruction to initiate and clarify major concepts and generalizations contained in the ensuing lesson, from the basal textbook. The basal stresses the scope and sequence of subject matter content to be emphasized in the curriculum. Within that framework, subject matter content is chosen for daily ensuing lessons. Generally, this follows the order of content presented in the basal. Which are relevant objectives of instruction in mathematics? The following, among others, are salient for pupils to attain in ongoing lessons and units of study :

- knowledge of symbols, formulas, graphs, and operations on number.
- number systems, place value, and key structural ideas.
- meaning of essential content in plane and solid geometry.
- rational and logical thinking.
- critical and creative thinking.
- problem solving and project methods of learning (National Council Teachers of Mathematics, 2006).

Both inductive and deductive methods may also be used. There can be considerable flexibility in methods used when the basal textbook serves as a guide in teaching mathematics. A teacher's manual accompanying the basal provides a listing of objectives for each lesson, learning activities to achieve objectives, and evaluation procedures to notice student progress. Diagnosis of pupil errors may also be inherent in the manual.

IN CLOSING

Any approved approach in teaching mathematics must be based upon sound principles of teaching and learning. Pupil interest needs to be fostered in ongoing lessons and units of study. Learners should be actively involved in achieving well in the mathematics curriculum. Meaning and understanding must accrue when vital concepts and generalizations are acquired. Pupil purpose is salient to develop as well as maintain. Thus, there must be reasons for achieving sequential objectives. Individual differences need to be provided for, among pupils.

There are disadvantages in using either CAI or Basal mathematics textbooks in teaching mathematics. For example, CAI may hinder social development of pupils since interaction with computers, not people is involved. Basal textbook use may become boring with sequential pages followed each day in teaching. It is advantageous to vary the methods and procedures of instruction to secure the benefits of using any one approach in teaching mathematics.

Mathematics teachers need to be concerned about the attitudes and feelings of students. There needs to be quality communication among teachers and students. Respect for each person in the school and classroom setting is important. Patience should be shown when students learn necessary skills in working with computers. Also, there needs to be a thorough understanding of what motivates pupils to achieve. Motivation is a key concept in learning (National Research Council 2001).

References

Djeassilane, N. (2008), "Effect of Computer Aided Instruction (CAI) in Enhancing the Academic Achievement of Higher Secondary Students in Commerce. Ph D thesis evaluated by the writer for Alagappa University, Karaikudi-630003, India.

Ediger, Marlow (2005), "Teaching Mathematics in the High School Setting," *College Student Journal*, 39 (4), 711-715.

Ediger, Marlow (2006) "Writing in the Mathematics Curriculum," *Journal of Instructional Psychology*, 33 (2), 120-123.

Ediger, Marlow, and D. Bhaskara Rao (2001), *Teaching Mathematics Successfully*. New Delhi, India : Discovery Publishing House.

National Council Teachers of Mathematics (1989), *Curriculum and Evaluation Standards for School Mathematics*. Reston, Virginia: NCTM.

National Council Teachers of Mathematics (2006), *Curriculum Focal Points for Kindergarten Through Grade Eight Mathematics: A Quest for Coherence*. Reston, Va. : NCTM.

National Research Council (2001), *Adding It Up. Helping Children Learn Mathematics*. Washington, DC: National Academy Press.

Wiske, S. (2004), "Use Technology to dig for Meaning," *Educational Leadership*, 63(1), 478.

16 CHAPTER

Reading in Mathematics Curriculum

There are selected procedures which may be used to assist students having difficulties in reading mathematics problems. Difficulties in reading should not hold students back from achieving more optimally in mathematics. Methods of helping students with reading problems and comprehension in mathematics will be discussed in this manuscript.

Analyzing Mathematical Reading Problems

Several procedures will be discussed. The teacher may immediately pronounce words to a student who fail in the identification process. This procedure has as its advantage in that students will not lose out on ideas read due to the almost immediate pronunciation of unknown words in context. However, the student may not retain these as sight words if no specific approach is learned in word recognition (Ediger, 2007).

Phonics might well assist students in reading an unknown word. The word "sum" is very consistent in spelling between symbol and sound. Phonics works very well in word identification when words reveal this consistency. With other words in mathematics, there is less consistency such as in the following: "greater" than, "inverse" operation, "regroup", "subtraction", among others. Even in these words there is some consistency as in "gr", (group), inverse without its "in" prefix, "regroup", with "re" prefix consistency between symbol and sound, as well as "subtraction" with "sub" letters, each making its very own consistent sound.

Irregularly spelled words may be recognized as following a pattern such as "tion" in the words subtraction, addition, division, and multiplication, making the ending sound of "shun". If phonics does not work in word recognition, then context clues might well assist. Thus, words must fit in meaningfully with the balance of the words in the sentence or paragraph. Sometimes, students fill in words which just do not make sense. The word must make for meaningful learning (Ediger, 1989).

Recognizing known syllables has many advantages in unlocking unknown words. If a student does not recognize a word, he/she may divide it into syllables for identification purposes, making the word(s) recognizable. The prefix "un" is used frequently as is the suffix "er". By removing a syllable, then, a pupil may identify a word correctly.

As a junior high school teacher, the writer in the latter fifties read aloud several word problems while struggling readers in a small group would follow along in their mathematics textbooks. This was done in an atmosphere of respect for all in the classroom. Struggling readers, generally could then proceed sequentially with the usual amount of supervision.

Reading Mathematics Problems Aloud

As a method of tackling problems in word recognition then, the writer read aloud selected story problems as the struggling readers followed along in their textbooks. In this way, learners were able to do the needed work in mathematics. Also, an opaque projector may be used to enlarge the print from the basal textbook so all can see clearly from their seats in a small group. The teacher may then read the words aloud as students follow along from the screen. Next, students may read aloud together with the teacher until the read aloud is successful and students understand what to do in mathematics. This approach does not embarrass any slow reader. Problems in reading should not interfere with achievement in mathematics. How did this assist learners?

- pupils developed a basic mathematics sight vocabulary from repeated reading
- pupils decide which words should then appear on a word wall, for review purposes
- pupils should comprehend the ideas well from the read aloud
- pupils develop a better self concept by not stumbling on word recognition problems (National Council Teachers of Mathematics, 1989).

Peer reading of word problems my also be emphasized. Thus, a proficient reader may read aloud to others who have difficulties in word recognition. In an atmosphere of respect, he/she needs to read aloud so that word identification does not hinder achievement in mathematics. The writer has noticed in classrooms whereby lay volunteers do a good job of helping students to decode and understand word problems. A conscientious Future Teachers of America high school club member has been observed to do a very good job of assisting struggling readers to identify unknown words (Ediger, 2007).

A variety of interesting procedures need to be used to assist struggling readers to identify unknown words. Methods of word recognition must be quickly implemented so that students secure the needed mathematical information sequentially to solve word problems. Being stuck on unknown words makes for feelings of failure. Sequence of ideas in reading then comes to a halt with frustration involved. Rather, assistance needs to be given quickly in word identification so that the learner may attend to solving mathematical problems, rather than struggling over unknown words.

There are salient principles of psychology which the mathematics teacher should use when assisting students in word recognition. These include the following :

- engaging students in learning rather than have passive recipients of knowledge
- providing adequate background information to students, prior to proceeding with the unknown
- emphasize meaning and understanding in teaching and learning situations
- stress interest factors in learning; avoid student boredom in achieving
- assist students to perceive purpose in identifying unknown words (Roy, 2009).

Providing for Individual Needs

Mathematics teachers need to provide for individual differences among students. Thus, needs vary from student to student. With diagnosis and remediation data, the teacher may assist each to achieve more optimally in mathematics. Mathematics must be taught from a developmental point of view, but this is not always possible. Thus, the teacher needs to analyze what pupils need and then strengthen these areas of concern.

Mathematics teachers need to ascertain where a pupil is achieving presently and then provide quality experiences which make for subsequent feelings of accomplishment. The materials of instruction used might well provide for individual styles of learning also, such as the utilization of :

- concrete objects and items to teach addition, subtraction, multiplication, and division, i.e. checkers used to show a set of five and set of three, joining the two sets to make a set of eight. The abstract numerals

"5 + 3 = 8" should accompany the concrete markers. Structural ideas including the commutative properly of addition and multiplication, the associative property of addition and multiplication. The inverse operation of subtraction and division may also be shown with concrete markers and the accompanying abstract numerals.

- semi-concrete materials to convey mathematical including pictures, illustrations, audio-visual aids, power point slides, teacher made felt cut outs and the flannel board, diagrams and drawings, and video tapes explaining salient mathematics procedures and processes
- abstract materials of instruction including the mathematics basal textbook, the number line, related worksheets and the accompanying workbook, computer use, as well as teacher developed materials (Kennedy and Tipps, 1991).

Each of the above must be adapted to individual pupil needs such as pupils reading content from pictures and illustrations in assisting pupils in learning to count drawings therein. Or, accompanying work book subject matter used to determine the area of a parallelogram.

Methods of teaching must match the learning styles of pupils, in general, and these include the following :

- inductive learning or learning by discovery in mathematics
- deductive learning through clearly provided explanations
- project methods as in developing a *product* such as a triangle, square, trapezoid, and rectangle from construction paper
- problem solving in which a small group or committee of pupils seek to find solutions to a lifelike mathematical problem whereby higher cognitive levels of thought are used in the process.

CONCLUSION

There are a variety of purposes involved in reading mathematical content. Word recognition and comprehension are two vital factors in reading mathematical subject matter. Pupils must attach meaning to what is being read so that they may work on the mathematical facets of computing, reasoning, and understanding.

References

Ediger, Marlow (2007), "Readiness for Mathematics Learning and the Student," *Experiments in Education*, 35 (8),1-5.

Ediger, Marlow (1989), "Psychology of Teaching Mathematics," *Delta K*, 27 (4), 20-23.

Ediger, Marlow (2007), "Meaning in Reading Instruction," *Reading Improvement*, 44(4), 217-220.

National Council Teachers of Mathematics (1989), *Curriculum and Evaluation Standards for School Mathematics*. Reston, Virginia: NCTM.

Roy, Ruma (2009), "New Challenges in Teacher Education, *Edutracks*, 8 (6), 19-20.

Kennedy, Leonard M., Tipps, Steve (1991), *Guiding Children's Learning of Mathematics*. Belmont, California: Wadsworth Publishing Company.

Additional Reading

Amala, P.A. and Anupama, P., Authors and Digumarti Bhaskara Rao, Editor (2004). *History of Education.* New Delhi : Discovery Publishing House. ISBN 81-7141-860-0.

Appala Naidu, P.Ch., Author and Digumarti Bhaskara Rao, Editor (2007). *Student Feedback Methods.* New Delhi : Discovery Publishing House.

Bhaskara Rao, Digumarti (1994). *Scientific Aptitude.* New Delhi : Ashish Publishing House. ISBN 81-7024-658-X.

Bhaskara Rao, Digumarti (1995). *Animal Kingdom.* New Delhi : Discovery Publishing House. ISBN 81-7141-274-2.

Bhaskara Rao, Digumarti (1995). *Batracology.* New Delhi : Discovery Publishing House. ISBN 81-7141-279-3.

Bhaskara Rao, Digumarti (1997). *Scientific Attitude.* New Delhi : Discovery Publishing House. ISBN 81-7141-381-1.

Bhaskara Rao, Digumarti (1996). *Scientific Attitude vis-à-vis Scientific Aptitude.* New Delhi : Discovery Publishing House. ISBN 81-7141-308-0.

Bhaskara Rao, Digumarti (2004). *Scientific Attitude, Scientific Aptitude and Achievement.* New Delhi : Discovery Publishing House. ISBN 81-7141-781-7.

Bhaskara Rao, Digumarti (2004). *Educational Administration.* New Delhi : Discovery Publishing House. ISBN 81-7141-842-2.

Bhaskara Rao, Digumarti (2004). *Issues in School Education.* New Delhi : Discovery Publishing House. ISBN 81-8356-025-3.

Bhaskara Rao, Digumarti, Editor (1996). *Encyclopaedia of Education For All,* 5 Volumes. New Delhi : APH Publishing Corporation. ISBN 81-7024-759-4 (set).

Vol. I *Education For All : The World Conference.* ISBN 81-7024-760-8.

Vol. II *Education For All : The EPA-9 Summit.* ISBN 81-7024-761-6.

Vol. II *Education For All : Quality Education For All*. ISBN 81-7024-762-6.

Vol. IV *Education For All : Planning and Monitoring*. ISBN 81-7024-763-4.

Vol. V *Education For All : The Indian Scenario*. ISBN 81-7024-764-0.

Bhaskara Rao, Digumarti, Editor (1999). *International Encyclopaedia of AIDS*, 11 Volumes. New Delhi: Discovery Publishing House. ISBN 81-7141-522-6 (set).

Vol. 1 *Introduction to HIV/AIDS*. ISBN 81-7141-523-7.

Vol. 2 *HIV/AIDS – Issues and Challenges*, 2 parts. ISBN 81-7141-524-5.

Vol. 3 *HIV/AIDS – Socio Economic Realities*. ISBN 81-7141-524-3.

Vol. 4 *HIV/AIDS – Law Ethics and Human Rights*, 2 parts. ISBN 81-7141-526-1.

Vol. 5 *AIDS and NGOs*. ISBN 81-7141-527-X.

Vol. 6 *AIDS and Home Care*. ISBN 81-7141-528-8.

Vol. 7 *STD Case Management*. ISBN 81-7141-529-6.

Vol. 8 *HIV/AIDS Prevention and Care – Teaching Modules for Nurses and Midwives*. ISBN 81-7141-530-X.

Vol. 9 *HIV Prevention Education for Educational Institutions*. ISBN 81-7141-531-8.

Vol.10 *Instructional Modules for AIDS Education*. ISBN 81-7141-532-6.

Vol.11 *School Health Education to prevent AIDS and STD – A Package for Curriculum Planners*. ISBN 81-7141-533-4.

Bhaskara Rao, Digumarti, Editor (2000). *International Encyclopaedia of Human Rights*, 7 Volumes in 13 Parts. New Delhi : Discovery Publishing House. ISBN 81-7141-567-9 (set).

Vol. 1 *International Instruments of Human Rights*, 2 Parts. ISBN 81-7141-569-4.

Vol. 2 *Regional Instruments of Human Rights*. ISBN 81-7141-604-7.

Vol. 3 *Human Rights and the United Nations*, 2 parts. ISBN 81-7141-605-5.

Vol. 4 *Fact Files of Human Rights*, 3 Parts. ISBN 81-7141-606-3.

Vol. 5 *Study Stories of Human Rights*, 3 parts. ISBN 81-7141-607-3.

Vol. 6 *International Meetings on Human Rights*, 2 parts. ISBN 81-714-608-X.

Vol. 7 *Professional Training in Human Rights*. ISBN 81-7141-609-8.

Bhaskara Rao, Digumarti, Editor (2000). *International Encyclopaedia of Science and Technology Education*, 11 Volumes. New Delhi : Discovery Publishing House. ISBN 81-7141-548-2 (set).

Vol. 1 *Science and Technology Education*. ISBN 81-7141-568-7.

Vol. 2 *Science Education in Developing Countries*. ISBN 81-7141-569-9.

Vol. 3 *Organizational Structure of Science*. ISBN 81-7141-570-9.

Vol. 4 *Science Education in Asia and the Pacific*. ISBN 81-7141-571-7

Vol. 5 *Science and Technology Education For All*. ISBN 81-7141-572-5.

Vol. 6 *Values, Ethics, Talent and Girls in Science and Technology Education*. ISBN 81-7141-573-3.

Vol. 7 *Popularization of Science and Technology Education*. ISBN 81-7141-574-1.

Vol. 8 *Science, Power and Society*. ISBN 81-7141- 575-X.

Vol. 9 *Information Technology*. ISBN 81-7141-576-8.

Vol.10 *Teacher Training in Science and Technology Education*. ISBN 81-7142-577-6.

Vol.11 *Teacher Training in Science and Technology : A Curriculum Framework*. ISBN 81-7141-578-4.

Bhaskara Rao, Digumarti, Editor (2000). *Education For All : Achieving the Goal*, 3 Volumes. New Delhi : APH Publishing Corporation. ISBN 81-7648-152-1 (set).

Vol. I *The Global Consensus*. ISBN 81-7648-155-6.

Vol. II *Mid-Decade Review Reports of Regional Seminars*. ISBN 81-7648-154-8.

Vol. III *Issues and Trends*. ISBN 81-7648-155-6.

Bhaskara Rao, Digumarti, Editor (2004). *International Encyclopaedia of Learning to Live Together*, 4 Volumes. New Delhi : Discovery Publishing House. ISBN 81-7141-848-1.

Vol. 1 *International Conference on Learning to Live Together*.

Vol. 2 *Globalization and Living Together*.

Vol. 3 *Curriculum for Learning to Live Together*.

Vol. 4 *Science Education for the Contemporary Society* .

Bhaskara Rao, Digumarti, Editor (2005). *Encyclopaedia of Education For All*, 3 Volumes. New Delhi : Discovery Publishing House. ISBN 81-7141-647-0 (Set).

Bhaskara Rao, Digumarti, Editor (2007). *Encyclopaedia of Teacher Education*, 4 Volumes. New Delhi : Discovery Publishing House. ISBN 81-8356-306-6 (Set).

Bhaskara Rao, Digumarti, Editor (2007). *Encyclopaedia of Edeucation for Living Together*, 4 Volumes. New Delhi : Discovery Publishing House. ISBN 81-7141-848-1 (Set).

Bhaskara Rao, Digumarti, Editor (1996). *National Policy on Education*, 2 Volumes. New Delhi: Anmol Publications Pvt. Ltd. ISBN 81-7488-323-1.

Bhaskara Rao, Digumarti, Editor (1996). *Global Perceptions on Peace Education*, 3 Volumes. New Delhi : Discovery Publishing House. ISBN 81-7141-319-6.

Bhaskara Rao, Digumarti, Editor (1997). *Education for the 21st Century.* New Delhi : Discovery Publishing House. ISBN 81-7141-389-7.

Bhaskara Rao, Digumarti, Editor (1997). *Reflections on Scientific Attitude.* New Delhi : Discovery Publishing House. ISBN 81-7141-319-6.

Bhaskara Rao, Digumarti, Editor (1997). *Success Story of a Primary Education Project.* New Delhi : APH Publishing Corporation. ISBN 81-7024-850-7.

Bhaskara Rao, Digumarti, Editor (1997). *World Food Summit.* New Delhi : Discovery Publishing House. ISBN 81-7141-386-2.

Bhaskara Rao, Digumarti, Editor (1997). *Care the Child*, 2 Volumes. New Delhi: Discovery Publishing House. ISBN 81-7141-394-3.

Bhaskara Rao, Digumarti, Editor (1998). *Earth Summit*, 2 Volumes. New Delhi : Discovery Publishing House. ISBN 81-7141-435-4.

Bhaskara Rao, Digumarti, Editor (1998). *Adolescence Education.* New Delhi : Discovery Publishing House. ISBN 81-7141-432-X.

Bhaskara Rao, Digumarti, Editor (1998). *Community and School Nutrition Education.* New Delhi : Discovery Publishing House. ISBN 81-7141-435-4.

Bhaskara Rao, Digumarti, Editor (1998). *District Primary Education Programme.* New Delhi: Discovery Publishing House. ISBN 81-7141-396-X.

Bhaskara Rao, Digumarti, Editor (1998). *National Policy on Education : Towards an Enlightened and Humane Society.* New Delhi : Discovery Publishing House. ISBN 81-7141-426-5.

Bhaskara Rao, Digumarti, Editor (1998). *Reforming School Education.* New Delhi : Discovery Publishing House. ISBN 81-7141-403-6.

Bhaskara Rao, Digumarti, Editor (1998). *Teacher Education in India.* New Delhi : Discovery Publishing House. ISBN 81-7141-406-0.

Bhaskara Rao, Digumarti, Editor (1998). *World Summit for Social Development.* New Delhi : Discovery Publishing House. ISBN 81-7141-420-6.

Bhaskara Rao, Digumarti, Editor (2001). *Nuclear Materials : Issues and Concerns*, 2 Volumes. New Delhi : Discovery Publishing House. ISBN 81-7141-611-X.

Bhaskara Rao, Digumarti, Editor (2001). *Distance Education in Different Countries.* New Delhi : APH Publishing Corporation. ISBN 81-7648-229-3.

Bhaskara Rao, Digumarti, Editor (2001). *Decentralised Management of Education : Management of Education in Panchayati Raj and Municipal Bodies.* New Delhi : Discovery Publishing House. ISBN 81-7141-617-9.

Bhaskara Rao, Digumarti, Editor (2001). *Electrochemistry for Environmental Protection.* New Delhi: Discovery Publishing House. ISBN 81-7141-619-5.

Bhaskara Rao, Digumarti, Editor (2001). *Global Educational Studies.* New Delhi : Discovery Publishing House. ISBN 81-7141-616-0.

Bhaskara Rao, Digumarti, Editor (2001). *Global Synthesis of Educational Assessment.* New Delhi : Discovery Publishing House. ISBN 81-7141-613-6.

Bhaskara Rao, Digumarti, Editor (2001). *Jomtein Decade of Education.* New Delhi : Discovery Publishing House. ISBN 81-7141-618-7.

Bhaskara Rao, Digumarti, Editor (2001). *World Conference on Education for All.* New Delhi: APH Publishing Corporation. ISBN 81-7141-274-9.

Bhaskara Rao, Digumarti, Editor (2001). *World Conference on Higher Education.* New Delhi : Discovery Publishing House. ISBN 81-7141-610-1.

Bhaskara Rao, Digumarti, Editor (2001). *World Conference on Science.* New Delhi : Discovery Publishing House. ISBN 81-7141-612-8.

Bhaskara Rao, Digumarti, Editor (2003). *Inspiring Experiences in Teacher Education.* New Delhi : Discovery Publishing House. ISBN 81-7141-656-X.

Bhaskara Rao, Digumarti, Editor (2003). *International Studies in Education*, 3 Volumes. New Delhi : Discovery Publishing House. ISBN 81-7141-647-0.

Bhaskara Rao, Digumarti, Editor (2003). *Military Conversion : Impact on Science and Technology.* New Delhi : Discovery Publishing House. ISBN 81-7141-578-4.

Bhaskara Rao, Digumarti, Editor (2003). *United Nations Millennium Summit.* New Delhi : Discovery Publishing House. ISBN 81-7141-632-2.

Bhaskara Rao, Digumarti, Editor (2003). *World Assembly on Aging.* New Delhi : Discovery Publishing House. ISBN 81-7141-637-3.

Bhaskara Rao, Digumarti, Editor (2003). *World Conference on Human Rights.* New Delhi: Discovery Publishing House. ISBN 81-7141-661-6.

Bhaskara Rao, Digumarti, Editor (2003). *World Education Forum.* New Delhi: Discovery Publishing House. ISBN 81-7141-639-X.

Bhaskara Rao, Digumarti, Editor (2003). *Education, Employment and Human Resource Development*. New Delhi : Discovery Publishing House. ISBN 81-7141- 681-0.

Bhaskara Rao, Digumarti, Editor (2003). *Successful Schooling*. New Delhi : Discovery Publishing House. ISBN 81-7141-677-2.

Bhaskara Rao, Digumarti, Editor (2003). *European Education and Teachers.* New Delhi: Discovery Publishing House. ISBN 81-7141-702-7.

Bhaskara Rao, Digumarti, Editor (2003). *Teachers in a Changing World.* New Delhi : Discovery Publishing House. ISBN 81-7141-694-2.

Bhaskara Rao, Digumarti, Editor (2004). *International Guidelines on Open and Distance Teacher Education*. New Delhi: Discovery Publishing House. ISBN 81-7141-777-9.

Bhaskara Rao, Digumarti, Editor (2004). *Adult Learning in the 21st Century.* New Delhi: Discovery Publishing House. ISBN 81-7141-797-3.

Bhaskara Rao, Digumarti, Editor (2004). *Educational Practices : Research and Recommendations*. New Delhi: Discovery Publishing House. ISBN 81-7141-835-X.

Bhaskara Rao, Digumarti, Editor (2004). *General Secondary Education In the 21st Century*. New Delhi: Discovery Publishing House.

Bhaskara Rao, Digumarti, Editor (2004). *Reforming Secondary Education.* New Delhi: Discovery Publishing House. ISBN 81-7141-843-0.

Bhaskara Rao, Digumarti, Editor (2004). *Human Rights Education.* New Delhi : Discovery Publishing House. ISBN 81-7141-882-1.

Bhaskara Rao, Digumarti, Editor (2004). *United Nations Decade for Human Rights Education.* New Delhi : Discovery Publishing House. ISBN 81-7141- 887-2.

Bhaskara Rao, Digumarti, Editor (2004). *Technical and Vocational Education and Training in the 21st Century.* New Delhi : Discovery Publishing House. ISBN 81-7141-984-4.

Bhaskara Rao, Digumarti, Editor (2005). *Encyclopaedia of Education For All,* 5 Volumes. New Delhi : Discovery Publishing House.

Bhaskara Rao, Digumarti and B.S.V. Dutt, Editors (2003). *Education : Programmes and Policies.* New Delhi : APH Publishing Corporation. ISBN 81-7648-470-9.

Bhaskara Rao, Digumarti, C.A.P. Swamy and B.S.V. Dutt (1997). *Self-Evaluation in Student Teaching.* New Delhi : Discovery Publishing House. ISBN 81-7141-374-9.

Bhaskara Rao, Digumarti and C.D. Swarna Lattha, Editors (2006). *Encyclopaedia of Biotechnology*, 5 Volumes. New Delhi : Discovery Publishing House. ISBN 81-8356-168-3 (set).

Bhaskara Rao, Digumarti, C. Sridevi and K. Vijaya (1995). *Achievement in Social Studies.* New Delhi: Discovery Publishing House. ISBN 81-7141-281-5.

Bhaskara Rao, Digumarti and D. Naresh Kumar (2004). *School Teacher Effectiveness.* New Delhi : Discovery Publishing House. ISBN 81-7141-782-5.

Bhaskara Rao, Digumarti and D. Sridhar (2002). *Job Satisfaction of School Teachers.* New Delhi : Discovery Publishing House. ISBN 81-7141-652-7.

Bhaskara Rao, Digumarti and Digumarti Pushpa Latha, Editors (1998). *International Encyclopaedia of Women*, 5 Volumes. New Delhi : Discovery Publishing House. ISBN 81-7141-410-9 (Set).

Vol. 1 *Status of World's Women*. ISBN 81-7141- 494-X.

Vol. 2 *Women, Education and Empowerment.* ISBN 81-7141-498-1.

Vol. 3 *Women Challenges and Advancement.* ISBN 81-7141-497-4.

Vol. 4 *Women and Family Health.* ISBN 81-7141- 497-4.

Vol. 5 *Women and International Action.* ISBN 81-7141-498-2.

Babu, P.C., Author and Digumarti Bhaskara Rao, Editor (2004). *Flowers of Wisdom.* New Delhi : Discovery Publishing House. ISBN 81-7141-695-0.

Babu, P.C., Author and Digumarti Bhaskara Rao, Editor (2008). *Worlds of Wisdom.* New Delhi: Discovery Publishing House.

Bhagya Lakshmi, L., Author and Digumarti Bhaskara Rao, Editor (2000). *Reading and Comprehension.* New Delhi : Discovery Publishing House. ISBN 81-7141-543-1.

Bhasha, S.A., Author and Digumarti Bhaskara Rao, Editor (2004). *Methods of Teaching Geography.* New Delhi : Discovery Publishing House. ISBN 81-7141-807-4.

Bhaskara Rao, Digumarti (1986). *Dhrushya Sravana Bodhanapakaranalu* (Audio Visual Teaching Aids). Guntur : Nagarjuna Publishers.

Bhaskara Rao, Digumarti (1993). *Jeevasashtra Bodhana* (Teaching of Biology). Guntur : Nagarjuna Publishers.

Bhaskara Rao, Digumarti (1994). *Vidya Manovignana Sastram* (Educational Psychology). Guntur : Nagarjuna Publishers.

Bhaskara Rao, Digumarti (1995). *Vignanasasthra Bodhana* (Teaching of science) Guntur : Nagarjuna Publishers.

Bhaskara Rao, Digumarti (1997). *Vidya Manovignana Sastram* (Educational Psychology). Guntur : Creative Press.

Bhaskara Rao, Digumarti (1998). *DSC Study Material.* Guntur : Nagarjuna Publishers.

Bhaskara Rao, Digumarti (1998). *Upadhyayudu Vidya.* (Teacher and Education) Guntur : Nagarjuna Publishers.

Bhaskara Rao, Digumarti (1998). *Vidya Drukpadalu* (Perspectives of Education). Guntur : Nagarjuna Publishers.

Bhaskara Rao, Digumarti (1999). *EdCET Teaching Aptitude.* Guntur : Nagarjuna Publishers.

Bhaskara Rao, Digumarti (2001). *Bharata Samajamulo Upadyayudu Vidhya* (Teacher and Education in Emerging Indian Society). Guntur : Sri Nagarjuna Publishers.

Bhaskara Rao, Digumarti (2001). *Bhoutika Sastra Bodhana Padhatulu* (Methods of Teaching Physical Science). Guntur : Sri Nagarjuna Publishers.

Bhaskara Rao, Digumarti (2001). *Jeeva Sastra Bodhana Padhatulu* (Methods of Teaching Biology). Guntur : Sri Nagarjuna Publishers.

Bhaskara Rao, Digumarti (2001). *Vidya Manovignana Sastram* (Educational Psychology). Guntur : Sri Nagarjuna Publishers.

Bhaskara Rao, Digumarti (2003). *Patasala Yajamanyam / Paripalana* (School Management and Administration). Guntur : Sri Nagarjuna Publishers.

Bhaskara Rao, Digumarti and A. Jagadish (2009). *Vignansastra Bodhana Padhatulu* (Methods of Teaching Science).Guntur : Sri Nagarjuna Publishers.

Bhaskara Rao, Digumarti and B. Prasad Babu (2009). *Pradhamika Vidya mariyu Vileena Vidya Dhrukpadhalu* (Perspectives in Primary Education and Inclusive Education). Guntur : Sri Nagarjuna Publishers.

Bhaskara Rao, Digumarti and B. Prasad Babu (2009). *Vidya Manovignana Sastram* (Educational Psychology). Guntur : Sri Nagarjuna Publishers.

Bhaskara Rao, Digumarti and D. Naresh Kumar (2004). *School Teacher Effectiveness.* New Delhi : Discovery Publishing House. ISBN 81-7141-782-5.

Bhaskara Rao, Digumarti and Digumarthi Harshitha (2004). *Adjustment of Adolescents.* New Delhi: APH Publishing House. ISBN 81-7648-836-8.

Bhaskara Rao, Digumarti and Digumarthi Harshitha, Editors (2001). *Education in India.* New Delhi: APH Publishing House. ISBN 81-7648-207-2.

Bhaskara Rao, Digumarti and Digumarti Pushpa Latha (1994). *Achievement in Biology*. New Delhi : Discovery Publishing House. ISBN 81-7141-264-5.

Bhaskara Rao, Digumarti and Digumarti Pushpa Latha (1994). *Achievement in Science*. New Delhi : Discovery Publishing House. ISBN 81-7141-280-70.

Bhaskara Rao, Digumarti and Digumarti Pushpa Latha (1995). *Achievement in English*. New Delhi : Discovery Publishing House. ISBN 81-7141-283-1.

Bhaskara Rao, Digumarti and Digumarti Pushpa Latha (1995). *Achievement in Mathematics*. New Delhi : Discovery Publishing House. ISBN 81-7141-278-5.

Bhaskara Rao, Digumarti and Digumarti Pushpa Latha (2004). *Education for Women*. New Delhi : Discovery Publishing House. ISBN 81-7141-873-2.

Bhaskara Rao, Digumarti and E. Sreekanth Babu (2004). *Educational Interests of School Students*. New Delhi : Discovery Publishing House. ISBN 81-7141-837-6.

Bhaskara Rao, Digumarti and G. Prasanthi (2009). *Samardya Nirmanamu* (Capacity Building). Guntur : Sri Nagarjuna Publishers.

Bhaskara Rao, Digumarti and K. Subba Rao (2009). *Elementary Vidya, Pranalika, Yajamanyam, Upadyaya Kartavyalu* (Elementary Education, Planning, Management and Teacher Functions). Guntur : Sri Nagarjuna Publishers.

Bhaskara Rao, Digumarti and K. Vijaya (1995). *A Text Book Evaluation*. Ambala Cantt : The Associated Publishers.

Bhaskara Rao, Digumarti and K.R.S. Sambasiva Rao, Editors (1996). *Current Trends in Indian Education*. New Delhi : Discovery Publishing House. ISBN 81-7141-311-0.

Bhaskara Rao, Digumarti and M.A. Fayaz (2004). *Problems of Primary School Drop-outs*. New Delhi : Discovery Publishing House. ISBN 81-7141- 834-1.

Bhaskara Rao, Digumarti and N.V.M. Mohana Rao (2002). *Problems of Mentally Handicapped Children*. New Delhi : Discovery Publishing House. ISBN 81-7141- 645-4.

Bhaskara Rao, Digumarti and S. Chandra Mohan (2002). *Sports Management*. New Delhi : APH Publishing House. ISBN 81-7648-467-9.

Bhaskara Rao, Digumarti and S.A. Khader (2004). *Problems of Private School Teachers*. New Delhi : Discovery Publishing Corporation. ISBN 81-7141-838-4.

Bhaskara Rao, Digumarti and S.A. Khader (2004). *School Education in India.* New Delhi : Discovery Publishing Corporation. ISBN 81-7141-849-X.

Bhaskara Rao, Digumarti and Sk. Johni Basha (2004). *Teachers' Population Education Awareness.* New Delhi : Discovery Publishing House. ISBN 81-7141-832-5.

Bhaskara Rao, Digumarti, Digumarthi Harshitha and K.R.S. Sambasiva Rao, Editors (1999). *Advanced Biotechnology.* New Delhi : Discovery Publishing House. ISBN 81-7141-516-4.

Bhaskara Rao, Digumarti, Digumarti Pushpa Latha and Digumarthi Harshitha, Editors (2001). *Biological Warfare.* New Delhi: Discovery Publishing House. ISBN 81-7141-597-0.

Bhaskara Rao, Digumarti, Digumarti Pushpa Latha and Digumarthi Harshitha, Editors (2001). *Women as Educators.* New Delhi: Discovery Publishing House. ISBN 81-7141-602-0.

Bhaskara Rao, Digumarti, Digumarti Pushpa Latha and Digumarthi Harshitha, Editors (2001). *Assessing Learning Achievement.* New Delhi: Discovery Publishing House. ISBN 81-7141-601-2.

Bhaskara Rao, Digumarti, Digumarti Pushpa Latha and Digumarthi Harshitha, Editors (2001). *Energy Security.* New Delhi : Discovery Publishing House. ISBN 81-7141-598-9.

Bhaskara Rao, Digumarti, Editor (2010). *Elementary Vidya, Pranalika, Yajamanyam, Upadyaya Kartavyalu – Question Bank* (Elementary Education, Planning, Management and Teacher Functions). Guntur: Sri Nagarjuna Publishers.

Bhaskara Rao, Digumarti, Editor (2010). *Ganithasastra Bodhana Padhatulu – Question Bank* (Methods of Teaching Science).Guntur : Sri Nagarjuna Publishers.

Bhaskara Rao, Digumarti, Editor (2010). *Methods of Teaching English – Question Bank.* Guntur : Sri Nagarjuna Publishers.

Bhaskara Rao, Digumarti, Editor (2010). *Pradhamika Vidya mariyu Vileena Vidya Dhrukpadhalu – Question Bank* (Perspectives in Primary Education and Inclusive Education). Guntur : Sri Nagarjuna Publishers.

Bhaskara Rao, Digumarti, Editor (2010). *Samardya Nirmanamu – Question Bank* (Capacity Building). Guntur : Sri Nagarjuna Publishers.

Bhaskara Rao, Digumarti, Editor (2010). *Sanghikasastra Bodhana Padhatulu – Question Bank* (Methods of Teaching Social Studies).Guntur : Sri Nagarjuna Publishers.

Bhaskara Rao, Digumarti, Editor (2010). *Telugu Bodhana Padhatulu – Question Bank* (Methods of Teaching Social Studies).Guntur: Sri Nagarjuna Publishers.

Bhaskara Rao, Digumarti, Editor (2010). *Vidya Manovignana Sastram – Question Bank* (Educational Psychology). Guntur : Sri Nagarjuna Publishers.

Bhaskara Rao, Digumarti, Editor (2010). *Vignansastra Bodhana Padhatulu – Question Bank* (Methods of Teaching Science).Guntur : Sri Nagarjuna Publishers.

Bhaskara Rao, Digumarti, N. Saraja, J. Lalitha and V. Mrunalini, Translators (2008). *Vidya – Samajam (Education - Society). Hyderabad* : Dr. B.R. Ambedkar Open University.

Bhaskara Rao, Digumarti, V.V. Rao, V.V. Lakshmi and V.V. Krishna, Editors (1999). *Status and Advancement of Women.* New Delhi: APH Publishing Corporation. ISBN 81-7648-169-6.

Bhuvaneswara Lakshmi, G. and K. Subba Rao, Authors and Digumarti Bhaskara Rao, Editor (2004). *Methods of Teaching Biology.* New Delhi : Discovery Publishing House. ISBN 81-7141-914-3.

Bhuvaneswara Lakshmi, G., Author and Digumarti Bhaskara Rao, Editor (2004). *Methods of Teaching Life Science.* New Delhi : Discovery Publishing House. ISBN 81-7141-804-X.

Bhuvaneswara Lakshmi, Gadde, Author and Digumarti Bhaskara Rao, Editor(2000). *Attitude Towards Science.* New Delhi: Discovery Publishing House. ISBN 81-7141-541-6.

Bujji Babu, K., Author and Digumarti Bhaskara Rao, Editor (2007). *Teaching Aptitude of Primary School Teachers.* New Delhi: Sonali Publications. ISBN 81-8411-083-9.

Chary, K.V.N.B., Author and Digumarti Bhaskara Rao, Editor (2006). *Techniques of Teaching Physics.* New Delhi : Sonali Publications. ISBN 81-8411-046-4.

Chowdary, S.B.J.R. and Naga Raju, Authors and Digumarti Bhaskara Rao, Editor (2004). *Mastery of Teaching Skills.* New Delhi : Discovery Publishing House. ISBN 81-7141-861-9

Dayakara Reddy, V. and Digumarti Bhaskara Rao, Editors (2006). *Value-Oriented Education.* New Delhi : Discovery Publishing House. ISBN 81-8356-051-2.

Devraj, T.A.S., Author and Digumarti Bhaskara Rao, Editor (1997). *Trace Analysis of Uranium and Thorium.* New Delhi : Discovery Publishing House. ISBN 81-7141-375-7.

Digumarti Bhaskara Rao and M. Srihari (2009). *Vardamana Bharata Desamulo Vidya* (Education in Emerging India). Guntur : Sri Nagarjuna Publishers.

Digumarti Bhaskara Rao, Editor (2010). *Vardamana Bharata Desamulo Vidya – Question Bank* (Education in Emerging India). Guntur : Sri Nagarjuna Publishers.

Durga Rani, K., Author and Digumarti Bhaskara Rao, Editor (2000). *Educational Aspirations and Scientific Attitudes.* New Delhi : Discovery Publishing House. ISBN 81-7141-555-5.

Dutt, B.S.V. and Digumarti Bhaskara Rao (2001). *Empowering Primary Teachers.* New Delhi : Discovery Publishing House. ISBN 81-7141-615-2.

Dutt, B.S.V., Author and Digumarti Bhaskara Rao, Editor (2004). *Comparative Education.* New Delhi: Discovery Publishing House. ISBN 81-7141-912-7.

Ediger, Marlow and Digumarti Bhaskara Rao (1996). *Science Curriculum.* New Delhi: Discovery Publishing House. ISBN 81-7141-321-8.

Ediger, Marlow and Digumarti Bhaskara Rao (2000). *Teaching Mathematics Successfully.* New Delhi : Discovery Publishing House. ISBN 81-7141-552-0.

Ediger, Marlow and Digumarti Bhaskara Rao (2001). *Teaching Science Successfully.* New Delhi : Discovery Publishing House. ISBN 81-7141-600-4.

Ediger, Marlow and Digumarti Bhaskara Rao (2001). *Teaching Social Studies Successfully.* New Delhi : Discovery Publishing House. ISBN 81-7141-596-2.

Ediger, Marlow and Digumarti Bhaskara Rao (2002). *Elementary Curriculum.* New Delhi : Discovery Publishing House. ISBN 81-7141-658-6.

Ediger, Marlow and Digumarti Bhaskara Rao (2002). *Improving School Administration.* New Delhi : Discovery Publishing House. ISBN 81-7141-633-0

Ediger, Marlow and Digumarti Bhaskara Rao (2002). *Philosophy and Curriculum.* New Delhi: Discovery Publishing House. ISBN 81-7141-631-4.

Ediger, Marlow and Digumarti Bhaskara Rao (2003). *Elementary Curriculum Improvement.* New Delhi : Discovery Publishing House. ISBN 81-7141-740-X.

Ediger, Marlow and Digumarti Bhaskara Rao (2003). *Language Arts Curriculum.* New Delhi : Discovery Publishing House. ISBN 81-7141-657-8.

Ediger, Marlow and Digumarti Bhaskara Rao (2003). *Psychology and Curriculum.* New Delhi : Discovery Publishing House. ISBN 81-7141-691-8.

Ediger, Marlow and Digumarti Bhaskara Rao (2003). *School Curriculum and Administration.* New Delhi : Discovery Publishing House. ISBN 81-7141-709-4.

Ediger, Marlow and Digumarti Bhaskara Rao (2003). *School Curriculum and Administration.* New Delhi : Discovery Publishing House. ISBN 81-7141-709-4.

Ediger, Marlow and Digumarti Bhaskara Rao (2003). *Teaching Language Arts Successfully.* New Delhi : Discovery Publishing House. ISBN 81-7141-678-0.

Ediger, Marlow and Digumarti Bhaskara Rao (2003). *Teaching Mathematics in Elementary Schools.* New Delhi : Discovery Publishing House. ISBN 81-7141-687-X.

Ediger, Marlow and Digumarti Bhaskara Rao (2003). *Teaching Science in Elementary Schools.* New Delhi: Discovery Publishing House. ISBN 81-7141-698-5.

Ediger, Marlow and Digumarti Bhaskara Rao (2004). *Relevancy in Elementary Curriculum.* New Delhi : Discovery Publishing House. ISBN 81-7141-845-9.

Ediger, Marlow and Digumarti Bhaskara Rao (2004). *School Organisation.* New Delhi : Discovery Publishing House. ISBN 81-7141-843-0.

Ediger, Marlow and Digumarti Bhaskara Rao (2005). *Quality School Education.* New Delhi : Discovery Publishing House. ISBN 81-8356-022-9.

Ediger, Marlow and Digumarti Bhaskara Rao (2006). *Administration of Schools.* New Delhi : Discovery Publishing House.

Ediger, Marlow and Digumarti Bhaskara Rao (2006). *Community College – Curriculum and Teaching.* New Delhi : Discovery Publishing House. ISBN 81-8356-053-9.

Ediger, Marlow and Digumarti Bhaskara Rao (2006). *Curriculum of School Subjects.* New Delhi : Discovery Publishing House.

Ediger, Marlow and Digumarti Bhaskara Rao (2006). *Curriculum Organisation.* New Delhi: Discovery Publishing House.

Ediger, Marlow and Digumarti Bhaskara Rao (2006). *Issues in School Curruculum.* New Delhi : Discovery Publishing House. ISBN 81-8356-052-0.

Ediger, Marlow and Digumarti Bhaskara Rao (2006). *Reading Curriculum and Instruction.* New Delhi : Discovery Publishing House.

Ediger, Marlow and Digumarti Bhaskara Rao (2006). *Successful School Education.* New Delhi : Discovery Publishing House. ISBN 81-8356-054-7.

Ediger, Marlow and Digumarti Bhaskara Rao (2006). *Successful School Administration.* New Delhi : Discovery Publishing House. ISBN 81-8356-046-6.

Ediger, Marlow and Digumarti Bhaskara Rao (2007). *Language Arts Education.* New Delhi : Discovery Publishing House. ISBN 81-8356-333-3.

Ediger, Marlow and Digumarti Bhaskara Rao (2007). *School Science Education.* New Delhi : Discovery Publishing House. ISBN 81-8356-352-X.

Ediger, Marlow and Digumarti Bhaskara Rao (2010). *Effective Schooling.* New Delhi : Discovery Publishing House. ISBN 978-81-8356-613-1.

Ediger, Marlow and Digumarti Bhaskara Rao (2010). *Effective School Curriculum.* New Delhi : Discovery Publishing House. ISBN 978-81-8356-585-1.

Ediger, Marlow and Digumarti Bhaskara Rao (2010). *Essays on Teaching Science.* New Delhi : Discovery Publishing House.

Ediger, Marlow and Digumarti Bhaskara Rao (2010). *Essays on Teaching Social Studies.* New Delhi : Discovery Publishing House.

Ediger, Marlow and Digumarti Bhaskara Rao (2010). *Essays on Teaching Reading.* New Delhi : Discovery Publishing House.

Ediger, Marlow and Digumarti Bhaskara Rao (2010). *Essays on Teaching Mathematics.* New Delhi : Discovery Publishing House.

Ediger, Marlow and Digumarti Bhaskara Rao (2010). *Essays on Teaching and Learning.* New Delhi : Discovery Publishing House.

Ediger, Marlow and Digumarti Bhaskara Rao, Editors (2006). *Encyclopaedia of School Education*, 5 Volumes. New Delhi : Discovery Publishing House. ISBN 81-8356-308-2 (set).

Ediger, Marlow and Digumarti Bhaskara Rao, Editors (2006). *Encyclopaedia of School Administration*, 4 Volumes. New Delhi : Discovery Publishing House. ISBN 81-8356-307-4 (set).

Ediger, Marlow and Digumarti Bhaskara Rao, Editors (2007). *Encyclopaedia of School Curriculum*, 10 Volumes. New Delhi : Discovery Publishing House. ISBN 81-8356-305-8 (set).

Ediger, Marlow and Digumarti Bhaskara Rao, Editors (2007). *Encyclopaedia of Teaching*, 8 Volumes. New Delhi : Discovery Publishing House. ISBN 81-8356-305-8 (set).

Ediger, Marlow, B.S.V. Dutt and Digumarti Bhaskara Rao (2003). *Teaching English Successfully.* New Delhi : Discovery Publishing House. ISBN 81-7141-707-8.

Elizabeth, M.E.S., Author and Digumarti Bhaskara Rao, Editor (2004). *Methods of Teaching English.* New Delhi : Discovery Publishing House. ISBN 81-7141-809-0.

Elizabeth, M.E.S., Author and Digumarti Bhaskara Rao, Editor (2004). *Acquisition of English Vocabulary.* New Delhi : Discovery Publishing House. ISBN 81-8356-075-X.

Fatima, Sk. and Digumarti Bhaskara Rao (2008). *Reasoning Ability of Adolescent Students.* New Delhi : Sonali Publications.

Fatima, Sk. Author and Digumarti Bhaskara Rao, Editor (2007). *Reasoning Ability of School Students.* New Delhi : Discovery Publishing House. ISBN 81-8356-330-9.

G.E.P. Sastry and G. Satya Narayana, Authors, Bhaskara Rao, Digumarti, Editor (2009). *Sanghikasastra Bodhana Padhatulu* (Methods of Teaching Social Studies).Guntur : Sri Nagarjuna Publishers.

Gopala Krishna, G., A. Rama Krishna, K. Subba Rao and Bhaskara Rao, Digumarti (2004). *Jeevasashtra Bodhana Padhatulu* (Methods of Teaching of Biological science). Guntur : Sri Nagarjuna Publishers.

Gopala Krishna, M., Author and Digumarti Bhaskara Rao, Editor (2007). *Techniques of Teaching Physical Education.* New Delhi : Sonali Publications. ISBN 81-8411-044-8.

Gopala Krishna, M., Author and Digumarti Bhaskara Rao, Editor (2007). *Techniques of Teaching Education.* New Delhi : Sonali Publications. ISBN 81-8411-062-6.

Harshitha, Digumarthi, Author and Digumarti Bhaskara Rao, Editor (2004). *Methods of Teaching Information Technology.* New Delhi : Discovery Publishing House. ISBN 81-7141-805-8.

Harshitha, Digumarthi, Author and Digumarti Bhaskara Rao, Editor (2007). *Techniques of Teaching Computer Science.* New Delhi : Sonali Publications. ISBN 81-8411-036-7.

Indira Devi, Author and J. Prasanth Kumar and Digumarti Bhaskara Rao, Editors (2004). *Values in Language Text Books.* New Delhi : Discovery Publishing House. ISBN 81-7141-833-3.

Jalaja Kumari, C., Author and Digumarti Bhaskara Rao, Editor (2004). *Methods of Teaching Educational Technology.* New Delhi : Discovery Publishing House. ISBN 81-7141-810-4.

Jalaja Kumari, C., Author and Digumarti Bhaskara Rao, Editor (2007). *Job Satisfaction of Teachers.* New Delhi : Discovery Publishing House.

Janardhan Reddy, B., Author and Digumarti Bhaskara Rao, Editor (2006). *Techniques of Teaching Sociology.* New Delhi : Sonali Publications. ISBN 81-8411-042-1.

Jayasree, K., Author and Digumarti Bhaskara Rao, Editor (1999). *Correlates of Socialisation.* New Delhi : Discovery Publishing House. ISBN 81-7141-517-2.

Jayasree, K., Author and Digumarti Bhaskara Rao, Editor (2004). *Methods of Teaching Science.* New Delhi : Discovery Publishing House. ISBN 81-7141-801-5.

John Babu, C., Author and T.J.R. Prasad, G.M. Madhukar and Digumarti Bhaskara Rao, Editors (2004). *Problem Solving in Mathematics.* New Delhi : APH Publishing Corporation. ISBN 81-7648-273-0.

Joseph Raju, B and G.A. Anitha, Authors and Digumarti Bhaskara Rao, Editor (2004). *Population Education.* New Delhi : Sonali Publications. ISBN 81-88836-31-3.

Krishna Murthy, V., K.S. Sudheer Reddy and Digumarti Bhaskara Rao (2004). *Vidya Manovignana Sastra Adharalu* (Foundations of Educational Psychology). Guntur : Sri Nagarjuna Publishers.

Krishna, G., Author and Digumarti Bhaskara Rao, Editor (2006). *Techniques of Teaching Physical Education.* New Delhi : Discovery Publishing House. ISBN 81-8411-044-8.

Kumar Raja, G., Author and Digumarti Bhaskara Rao, Editor (2007). *Principles of Primary School.* New Delhi : Sonali Publications. ISBN 81-8411-054-5.

Lakshmi Kumari, V., Author and Digumarti Bhaskara Rao, Editor (2006). *Techniques of Teaching Home Science.* New Delhi : Discovery Publishing House. ISBN 81-8411-048-0.

Lalini, V., V. Dayakara Reddy, M. Srihari and Digumarti Bhaskara Rao (2004). *Vidya Adharalu* (Foundations of Education). Guntur : Sri Nagarjuna Publishers.

Lalitha, T., Author and K.S. Prabhakaram, D.S.N. Sastry and Digumarti Bhaskara Rao, Editors (2004). *Educational Philosophic Beliefs.* New Delhi: Discovery Publishing House. ISBN 81-7141-765-5.

Madhava, K., Author and Digumarti Bhaskara Rao, Editor (2008). *Personality of Adolescent Students.* New Delhi: Sonali Publications.

Madhu Bala, Jampala, Author and Digumarti Bhaskara Rao, Editor (2004). *Methods of Teaching Exceptional Children.* New Delhi: Discovery Publishing House. ISBN 81-7141-802-3.

Madhu Bala, Jampala, Author and Digumarti Bhaskara Rao, Editor (2007). *Adjustment, Achievement Motivation and Academic Achievement of Hearing Impaired Students.* New Delhi: Discovery Publishing House

Marja, Talvi and Digumarti Bhaskara Rao, Editors (1996). *Educational Leadership and Social Changes.* New Delhi : Discovery Publishing House. ISBN 81-7141-320-X.

Marlow Ediger and Digumarti Bhaskara Rao, Editors (2006). *Encyclopaedia of School Education*, 5 Volumes. New Delhi : Discovery Publishing House. ISBN 81-8356-308-2 (Set).

Marlow Ediger and Digumarti Bhaskara Rao, Editors (2006). *Encyclopaedia of School Administration*, 4 Volumes. New Delhi : Discovery Publishing House. ISBN 81-8356-307-4 (set).

Marlow Ediger and Digumarti Bhaskara Rao, Editors (2007). *Encyclopaedia of School Curriculum*, 10 Volumes. New Delhi : Discovery Publishing House. ISBN 81-8356-305-8 (set).

Marlow Ediger and Digumarti Bhaskara Rao, Editors (2007). *Encyclopaedia of Teaching*, 8 Volumes. New Delhi : Discovery Publishing House. ISBN 81-8356-305-8 (set).

Naga Kumari, U., Author and Digumarti Bhaskara Rao, Editor (2008). *Science Process Skills of School Students*. New Delhi : Sonali Publications.

Nageswara Rao, S. and M. Srihari, Authors and Digumarti Bhaskara Rao, Editor (2004). *Guidance and Counselling*. New Delhi : Discovery Publishing House. ISBN 81-7141-840-6.

Nageswara Rao, S. and P. Sridhar, Authors and Digumarti Bhaskara Rao, Editor (2004). *Methods and Techniques of Teaching*. New Delhi : Sonali Publications. ISBN 81-88836-33-8.

Nageswara Rao, S., Author and Digumarti Bhaskara Rao, Editor (2006). *Techniques of Teaching Psychology*. New Delhi : Discovery Publishing House. ISBN 81-8411-040-5.

Nirmala Jyothi, M., Author and Digumarti Bhaskara Rao, Editor (2003). *Non-detention System in School Education*. New Delhi : Discovery Publishing House. ISBN 81-7141-654-3.

Padma Tulasi, G., Author and Digumarti Bhaskara Rao, Editor (2004). *Methods of Teaching Elementary Science*. New Delhi : Discovery Publishing House. ISBN 81-7141-871-6.

Pala Prasada Rao, V., Author and D. Bhaskara Rao, Editors (2008). *Functioning of Autonomous Colleges*. New Delhi : Sonali Publications.

Pala Prasada Rao, V., Author and K. N. Rani and D. Bhaskara Rao, Editors (2004).*India Pakistan : Partition Perspectives in Indo English Novels*. New Delhi: Discovery Publishing House. ISBN 81-7141-871-6.

Pitchi Reddy, M., Author and Digumarti Bhaskara Rao, Editor (2007). *Techniques of Teaching Social Sciences*. New Delhi : Sonali Publications. ISBN 81-8411-066-X.

Prabhakaram, K.S., Author and Digumarti Bhaskara Rao, Editors (1998). *Concept Attainment Model in Mathematics Teaching*. New Delhi : Discovery Publishing House. ISBN 81-7141-424-9.

Prasad Babu, B., Author and M.V.R. Raju and Digumarti Bhaskara Rao, Editors (2006). *Behavioural Problems of School Children*. New Delhi: Discovery Publishing House. ISBN 81-8356-206-X.

Prasad Babu, B., Author and P. Madhu and Digumarti Bhaskara Rao, Editors (2006). *Psychological Adjustment and Well-being*. New Delhi: Discovery Publishing House. ISBN 81-8356-204-3.

Prasanth Kumar, J., Author and Digumarti Bhaskara Rao, Editor (1998). *Effectiveness of Distance Education System*. New Delhi : Discovery Publishing House. ISBN 81-7141-437-0.

Prasanth Kumar, J., Author and Digumarti Bhaskara Rao, Editor (2004). *Methods of Teaching Civics*. New Delhi : Discovery Publishing House. ISBN 81-7141-806-6.

Prasanth Kumar, J., Author and G. Sundara Rao and Digumarti Bhaskara Rao, Editors (2000). *Open University Student Support Services*. New Delhi : Discovery Publishing House. ISBN 81-7141-550-4.

Raja Kumari, M.A. and D.R.S. Sundari, Authors and Digumarti Bhaskara Rao, Editor (2004). *Special Education*. New Delhi : Discovery Publishing House. ISBN 81-7141-846-5.

Raja Kumari, M.A. and D.R.S. Sundari, Authors and Digumarti Bhaskara Rao, Editor (2004). *Methods of Teaching Educational Psychology*. New Delhi : Discovery Publishing House. ISBN 81-7141-820-1.

Rama Krishna Prasad and P. Vide Sagar, Authors and Digumarti Bhaskara Rao, Editor (2004). *Methods of Teaching Physical Education*. New Delhi: Discovery Publishing House.

Rama Krishnaiah, D., Author and Digumarti Bhaskara Rao, Editor (1998). *Job Satisfaction of College Teachers*. New Delhi : Discovery Publishing House. ISBN 81-7141-438-9.

Rama Kumar Ratnam, M.V., Author and Digumarti Bhaskara Rao, Editor (1998). *Dukkha : Suffering in Early Buddhism*. New Delhi: Discovery Publishing House. ISBN 81-7141-653-5.

Rama Seshaiah, P. Author and Digumarti Bhaskara Rao, Editor (2004). *Methods of Teaching Home Science*. New Delhi : Discovery Publishing House. ISBN 81-7141-916-X.

Rama Swamy, K., Author and Digumarti Bhaskara Rao, Editor (2007). *Techniques of Teaching Environmental Science*. New Delhi : Sonali Publications. ISBN 81-8411-035-9.

Ramatulasamma, K., Author and Digumarti Bhaskara Rao, Editor (2002). *Job Satisfaction of Teacher Educators.* New Delhi : Discovery Publishing House. ISBN 81-7141-655-1.

Ramesh, A.R., Author and Digumarti Bhaskara Rao, Editor (2006). *Techniques of Teaching Commerce.* New Delhi : Sonali Publications. ISBN 81-8411-043-X.

Ramesh, Ghanta and Digumarti Bhaskara Rao, Editors (1998). *Environmental Education : Problems and Prospects.* New Delhi: Discovery Publishing House. ISBN 81-7141-423-0.

Ranga Rao, B., Author and Digumarti Bhaskara Rao, Editor (2007). *Techniques of Teaching Economics.* New Delhi : Sonali Publications. ISBN 81-8411-056-1.

Ranga Rao, R., Author and Digumarti Bhaskara Rao, Editor (2004). *Methods of Teacher Teaching.* New Delhi : Discovery Publishing House. ISBN 81-7141-812-0.

Rani, S.S., Author and Digumarti Bhaskara Rao, Editor (2006). *Techniques of Teaching Botany.* New Delhi : Discovery Publishing House. ISBN 81-8411-037-5.

Rathaiah, Lavu and Digumarti Bhaskara Rao (1997). *Achievement Correlates.* New Delhi: Discovery Publishing House. ISBN 81-7141-385-4.

Rathaiah, Lavu and Digumarti Bhaskara Rao, Editors (1996), *International Innovations in Education.* New Delhi : Discovery Publishing House. ISBN 81-7141-359-5.

Ravi Krishna, M., Author and Digumarti Bhaskara Rao, Editor (2004). *Examination System.* New Delhi : Discovery Publishing House. ISBN 81-7141-824-4.

Ravi Kumar, M., Author and Digumarti Bhaskara Rao, Editor (2004). *Methods of Teaching Computer Science.* New Delhi : Discovery Publishing House. ISBN 81-7141-823-6.

Rudramamba, B. and V. Lakshmi Kumari, Authors and Digumarti Bhaskara Rao, Editor (2004). *Methods of Teaching Economics.* New Delhi : Discovery Publishing House. ISBN 81-7141-900-3.

Rudramamba, B., Author and Digumarti Bhaskara Rao, Editor (2003). *Problems of Teaching.* New Delhi : APH Publishing Corporation. ISBN 81-7648-462-8.

Sambasiva Rao, P., Author and Digumarti Bhaskara Rao, Editor (2007). *Techniques of Teaching Psychology.* New Delhi : Sonali Publications. ISBN 81-8411-040-5.

Sanjeeva Rao, P.C., Author and Digumarti Bhaskara Rao, Editor (1996). *A Text Book of Geology.* New Delhi : Discovery Publishing House. ISBN 81-7141-313-7.

Santhanam, T., B. Prasad Babu and S. Sugandhi, Authors and Digumarti Bhaskara Rao, Editor (2007). *Children with Learning Disabilities.* New Delhi : Sonali Publications. ISBN 81-8411-077-4.

Santhanam, T., B. Prasad Babu and S. Sugandhi, Authors and Digumarti Bhaskara Rao, Editor (2008). *Learning Disabilities and Remedial Programmes.* New Delhi : Discovery Publishing House.

Sarala, M.M.O., Author and Digumarti Bhaskara Rao, Editor (2006). *Techniques of Teaching English.* New Delhi : Sonali Publications. ISBN 81-8411-047-2.

Satya Narayana, G., Author and Digumarti Bhaskara Rao, Editor (2008). *Attitude towards Social Studies and Achievement in Social Studies.* New Delhi : Sonali Publications.

Satya Narayana, P.V.V. and G. Krishna, Authors and Digumarti Bhaskara Rao, Editor (2004). *Curriculum Development and Management.* New Delhi : Discovery Publishing House. ISBN 81-7141-813-9.

Satya Narayana, V., Author and Digumarti Bhaskara Rao, Editor (2001). *Physical Education, Social Attitudes and Leadership Qualities.* New Delhi: Discovery Publishing House. ISBN 81-7141-593-8.

Shamsuddin, Sk. and V. Dayakara Reddy, Authors and Digumarti Bhaskara Rao, Editor (2007). *Academic Achievement and Values.* New Delhi : Discovery Publishing House.

Singh, Y.C., Author and Digumarti Bhaskara Rao, Editor (2006). *Techniques of Teaching Science.* New Delhi : Sonali Publications. ISBN 81-8411-041-3.

Sirisha Rani, S., Author and Digumarti Bhaskara Rao, Editor (2007). *Techniques of Teaching Botany.* New Delhi : Sonali Publications. ISBN 81-8411-037-5.

Siva Lakshmi, G.V. and G.L. Subbaiah, Authors and Digumarti Bhaskara Rao, Editor (2004). *Methods of Teaching Environmental Science.* New Delhi: Discovery Publishing House. ISBN 81-7141-839-2.

Sivaratnam Reddy, M., Author and Digumarti Bhaskara Rao, Editor (2004). *Creativity in College Students.* New Delhi : Discovery Publishing House. ISBN 81-7141-697-7.

Srihari, M., Author and Digumarti Bhaskara Rao, Editor (2003). *Values of Prospective Teachers.* New Delhi : Discovery Publishing House. ISBN 81-8356-328-7.

Srinivas Rao, P., Author and Digumarti Bhaskara Rao, Editor (2007). *Principles of Secondary School.* New Delhi : Sonali Publications. ISBN 81-8411-058-8.

Srinivas, G. and Digumarti Bhaskara Rao (2007). *Anxiety of Prospective Teachers.* New Delhi : Sonali Publications. ISBN 81-8411-084-7.

Srinivas, M. and I. Prasada Rao, Authors and Digumarti Bhaskara Rao, Editor (2004). *Methods of Teaching History.* New Delhi : Discovery Publishing House. ISBN 81-7141-803-1.

Srinivasa Rao, Mandalapu, Author and Digumarti Bhaskara Rao, Editor (2003). *Achievement Motivation and Achievement in Mathematics.* New Delhi : Discovery Publishing House. ISBN 81-7141-674-8.

Srinivasulu Reddy, M. and K.R.S. Sambasiva Rao, Authors and Digumarti Bhaskara Rao, Editor (1999). *A Text Book of Aquaculture.* New Delhi : Discovery Publishing House. ISBN 81-7141-482-6.

Subba Rao, K., Author and Digumarti Bhaskara Rao, Editor (2007). *School Education Policy.* New Delhi : Discovery Publishing House. ISBN 81-8356-285-X.

Subba Rao, K., Author and Digumarti Bhaskara Rao, Editor (2007). *Education Planning.* New Delhi : Sonali Publications. ISBN 81-8411-053-7.

Subba Rao, K.P., P. Ayodhya and Digumarti Bhaskara Rao (2004). *Patasala Yajamanyam – Vidhya Vyavasthalu* (School Management and Systems of Education). Guntur : Sri Nagarjuna Publishers.

Sudhakar Reddy, Y., Author and Digumarti Bhaskara Rao, Editor (2003). *Creativity in Adolescents.* New Delhi : Discovery Publishing House. ISBN 81-7141-659-4.

Sudhakar, V., B. Ravindra Babu, D.S. Kumar and Digumarti Bhaskara Rao (2004). *Vidya Sanketika Sastram - Computer Vidhya* (Educational Technology and Computer Education). Guntur : Sri Nagarjuna Publishers.

Suneetha, G., Author and Digumarti Bhaskara Rao, Editor (2004). *Environmental Awareness of School Students.* New Delhi : Sonali Publications. ISBN 81-8411-085-5.

Sunil Kumar, K. and K. Rama Krishana, Authors and Digumarti Bhaskara Rao, Editor (2004). *Methods of Teaching Chemistry.* New Delhi : Discovery Publishing House. ISBN 81-7141-913-5.

Sunita, E. and R. Sambasiva Rao, Authors and Digumarti Bhaskara Rao, Editor (2004). *Methods of Teaching Mathematics.* New Delhi : Discovery Publishing House. ISBN 81-7141-915-1.

Surya Madhava, I., Author and Digumarti Bhaskara Rao, Editor (2006). *Techniques of Teaching Geography.* New Delhi : Discovery Publishing House. ISBN 81-8411-034-0.

Surya Madhava, I., Author and Digumarti Bhaskara Rao, Editor (2007). *Techniques of Teaching Political Science.* New Delhi : Discovery Publishing House. ISBN 81-8411-061-8.

Swamy, K.R., Author and Digumarti Bhaskara Rao, Editor (2006). *Techniques of Teaching Environmental Science.* New Delhi : Discovery Publishing House. ISBN 81-8411-035-9.

Swarna Jyothi, K., Author and Digumarti Bhaskara Rao, Editor (2007). *Educational Research.* New Delhi : Sonali Publications. ISBN 81-8411-063-4.

Swarna Latha, C.D., and Digumarti Bhaskara Rao, Editors (2006). *Encyclopaedia of Biotechnology,* 5 Volumes. New Delhi : Discovery Publishing House. ISBN 81-8356-168-3.

Swarupa Rani, T. and J.R. Priyadarshini, Authors and Digumarti Bhaskara Rao, Editor (2004). *Educational Measurement and Evaluation.* New Delhi: Discovery Publishing House. ISBN 81-7141-859-7.

Valeri V. Koustiouk, Author and Digumarti Bhaskara Rao, Editor (2002). *A Text Book of Cryogenics.* New Delhi : Discovery Publishing House. ISBN 81-7141-642-X.

Vamsi Krishna, V., Author and Digumarti Bhaskara Rao, Editor (2004). *School Psychology.* New Delhi: Discovery Publishing House. ISBN 81-7141-880-5.

Vanaja, M. and N. Sneha Latha, Authors and Digumarti Bhaskara Rao, Editor (2004). *Student Shyness.* New Delhi : APH Publishing Corporation.

Vanaja, M., Author and Digumarti Bhaskara Rao, Editor (1999). *Inquiry Training Model.* New Delhi : Discovery Publishing House. ISBN 81-7141-515-6.

Vanaja, M., Author and Digumarti Bhaskara Rao, Editor (2004). *Methods of Teaching Physics.* New Delhi : Discovery Publishing House. ISBN 81-7141-867-8

Veena Kumari, Balusu and Digumarti Bhaskara Rao (1996). *Operation Black Board.* New Delhi : APH Publishing Corporation. ISBN 81-7024-711-X.

Veena Kumari, Balusu, Author and Digumarti Bhaskara Rao, Editor (2004). *Methods of Teaching Social Studies.* New Delhi : Discovery Publishing House. ISBN 81-7141-899-6.

Veena Kumari, Balusu, Author and Digumarti Bhaskara Rao, Editor (2000). *Psycho-Social Correlates of Achievement.* New Delhi : Discovery Publishing House. ISBN 81-7141-547-4.

Venkata Rao, B., Author and Digumarti Bhaskara Rao, Editor (2007). *Techniques of Teaching Chemistry.* New Delhi : Sonali Publications. ISBN 81-8411-057-X.

Venkata Rao, P. and Digumarti Bhaskara Rao (1989). *A Text Book of Zoology – Junior Intermediate.* Guntur : Vignan Publishers.

Venkata Rao, P. and Digumarti Bhaskara Rao (1989). *A Text Book of Zoology – Senior Intermediate.* Guntur : Vignan Publishers.

Venkateswara Rao, V., Author and Digumarti Bhaskara Rao, Editor (2004). *Problems of Education.* New Delhi : Discovery Publishing House. ISBN 81-7141-841-4.

Venkateswara Rao, V., V. Vijaya Lakshmi and V. Vamsi Krishna, Authors and Digumarti Bhaskara Rao, Editor (2004). *Education For All.* New Delhi : Sonali Publications. ISBN 81-88836-30-3.

Venkateswara Rao, V., V. Vijaya Lakshmi and V. Vamsi Krishna, Authors and Digumarti Bhaskara Rao, Editor (2004). *Education in India.* New Delhi : Sonali Publications. ISBN 81-88836-858-9.

Venkateswara Reddy, L. and Narayana, M. L, Authors and Digumarti Bhaskara Rao, Editor (2004). *Methods of Teaching Rural Sociology.* New Delhi : Discovery Publishing House. ISBN 81-7141-811-2.

Venkateswara Reddy, L. and Narayana, M. L., Authors and Digumarti Bhaskara Rao, Editor (2004). *Education for Dalits.* New Delhi : Discovery Publishing House. ISBN 81-7141-872-4.

Venkateswarlu, K. and S.J. Basha, Authors and Digumarti Bhaskara Rao, Editor (2004). *Methods of Teaching Commerce.* New Delhi : Discovery Publishing House. ISBN 81-7141-808-2.

Venugopala Rao, K., Author and Digumarti Bhaskara Rao, Editor (2000). *Teacher Morale in Secondary Schools.* New Delhi : Discovery Publishing House. ISBN 81-7141-551-2.

Venugopala Rao, K., Author and Digumarti Bhaskara Rao, Editor (2007). *Techniques of Teaching history.* New Delhi : Sonali Publications. ISBN 81-8411-059-6.

Vidya, C., Author and Digumarti Bhaskara Rao, Editor (1996). *A Text Book of Nutrition.* New Delhi : Discovery Publishing House. ISBN 81-7141-309-9.

Vijaya Bharathi, D., Author and Digumarti Bhaskara Rao, Editor (2000). *Educational Philosophies of Swami Vivekananda and John Dewey.* New Delhi : APH Publishing House. ISBN 81-7648-309-9.

Vijaya Bharathi, D., Author and Digumarti Bhaskara Rao, Editor (2005). *Educational Philosophy of John Dewey.* New Delhi : Discovery Publishing House. ISBN 81-8356-024-5.

Vijaya Bharathi, D., Author and Digumarti Bhaskara Rao, Editor (2005). *Educational Philosophy of Swami Vivekananda.* New Delhi : Discovery Publishing House. ISBN 81-8356-023-7.

Vijaya Kumar, S.J., Author and Digumarti Bhaskara Rao, Editor (2006). *Techniques of Teaching Mathematics.* New Delhi : Sonali Publications. ISBN 81-8411-039-1.

Vijaya Lakshmi, D., Author and Digumarti Bhaskara Rao, Editor (2004) *Basic Education.* New Delhi : Discovery Publishing House. ISBN 81-7141-881-3.

Vijaya Lakshmi, V., Author and Digumarti Bhaskara Rao, Editor (2006). *Techniques of Teaching Music.* New Delhi : Discovery Publishing House. ISBN 81-8411-038-3.

Vimala, T.D., B. Prasad Babu and Digumarti Bhaskara Rao, Editors (2007). *Stress, Coping and Management.* New Delhi : Sonali Publications. ISBN 81-8411-086-3.

Visalakshi, V., Author and Digumarti Bhaskara Rao, Editor (2006). *Techniques of Teaching Biology.* New Delhi : Sonali Publications. ISBN 81-8411-045-6.

Visalakshi, V., Author and Digumarti Bhaskara Rao, Editor (2007). *Techniques of Teaching Zoology.* New Delhi : Sonali Publications. ISBN 81-8411-055-3.

Index

A

Achievement, 9-10, 71-77

Adult, 96

Alternative forms, 68

B

Basal mathematics textbooks, 97

Basal textbook, 49, 96, 90

Bounce of the heads, 28

C

Clarity of ideas, 46

Clarity, 14

Classroom/school environment, 56

Clues, 48

Collaboration in improving mathematics curriculum, 65-70

Collaboration, 65

Communication, 2

Computer-aided instruction (CAI), 92

- in mathematics curriculum, 92-98
- programmes, 94

Computer programmes, 89

Confidence, 88

Constructivism, 33-38, 81-83

- in the mathematics curriculum, 62-63

Constructivists, 62

Cooperating teachers, 73

Curriculum improvement, 65-70

D

Data driven decision-making in mathematics, 59-64

- constructivism in the mathematics curriculum, 62-63
- testing to notice achievement, 59-61

Deliberation and thought, 81

Dewey, 81-83

Diagnosis and prescription, 95

Diagnosis and remediation data, 102

Direct teaching vs constructivism in mathematics, 33-38

- constructivism in teaching mathematics, 35-37
- direct teaching of mathematics, 33-35

E

Ediger, 2, 17, 22, 43, 53, 54, 55

Egg, 96

Egyptian system of numeration, 75

Encouragement, 73

English Language Learners (ELL), 18, 75

Enjoyment in mathematics curriculum, 85-91
- affective dimension in teaching and learning, 85-90
- what to avoid, 90
  - criticism of pupils, 90
  - impatience, 90
  - rudeness and rude comments, 90

F

Face validity, 68

Factors that assist mathematics achievement, 71-77
- class size and learner progress, 71-73
- evaluation of achievement, 75-76
- inservice growth, 73-75

Focal point of instruction, 85

G

Games, 90

Geoboards, 80

Good attitudes, 23, 32

Good teaching, 10

Growth and achievement, 73

I

Illustrations, 54

Inservice education and the substitute teacher, 39-42

Inservice education for substitute teachers, 42-43

Internet courses, 25

K

Kasinath, 78

Knowledge, 3

L

Larva, 96

M

Mathematical facets of computing, reading and understanding, 104

Mathematics curriculum and psychology of learning, 45-52
- guiding pupil mathematics learning, 50-52
- metacognition needs to be stressed in mathematics, 49-50
- teaching in a pupil centred mathematics programme, 45-49

Mathematics, 1-6
- attitudinal dimension in teaching mathematics, 5-6
- teaching of mathematics, 1-5

Metacognition, 49-50

Methods of teaching, 25

Mistakes, 63

Motivation, 97

N

National Council Teachers of Mathematics, 1989, 4, 16, 25, 29, 73, 95

National Research Council, 2001, 97

Newton, 60

O

Order and sequence, 89

P

Phonics, 99

Piaget, Jean, 51, 62, 81-83

Pitfalls, 90

Plethora, 33

Portfolios in mathematics curriculum, 78-84

- constructivism, 81-83
- Dewey, 81-83
- philosophy of portfolio development, 79-81
- Piaget, 81-83
- Vygotsky, 81-83

Principles of psychology, 102

Problem solving, 103

Problems in teaching mathematics, 20-26

- mathematics teacher must have thorough knowledge and skill in teaching and learning situations, 20
- seven problems in guiding pupil achievement and progress, 20-25

Psychological foundations in teaching mathematics, 7-13

- attitudes and student mathematics achievement, 9-10
- cooperative learning in mathematics, 10-11
- reasons for lack of student achievement, 7-9

Psychology of learning, 45-52

Pupa, 96

Q

Quality in mathematics curriculum, 53-58

- providing for individual differences in mathematics, 53-57

Quality teaches, 2

Quality teaching in mathematics, 27-32

- attitudinal development, 31-32
- teaching and learning in mathematics, 27-31

R

Readiness, 94

Reading in mathematics curriculum, 99-104

- analyzing mathematical reading problems, 99-100
- providing for individual needs, 102-103
- reading mathematics problems aloud, 100-102

Relevant, 66

Reliability, 60, 68

Remediation methods of teaching, 35

Remedying deficiencies, 90

Roman system of numeration, 75

Rudeness, 17

Russian psychologist, 51

S

Savithiri, 9

Scaffolding, 28, 36

Self-efficiacy, 10

Sequence of ideas in reading, 101

Skills, 26

Social theory of learning, 11

Standards of quality, 74

Struggling readers, 100

Student and computerized instruction, 92-97

Substitute teacher and mathematics curriculum, 39-44

T

Table of Contents, 79

Tangrams, 80

Trends in teaching mathematics, 14-19

innovation in the mathematics curriculum, 14-18

Trust, 74

V

Vygotsky, 11, 21, 81-83

W

Word problem, 47, 62, 101

Word recognition and comprehension, 104

Z

Zone of proximal development, 36